THE
What Investment

a-z
Guide to the
STOCK
EXCHANGE

THE
What Investment
a-z
Guide to the
STOCK
EXCHANGE

Juliet Oxborrow

with

Tom Winnifrith

B T BATSFORD LONDON
Batsford Business Books Online: www.batsford.com

©B T Batsford Ltd
First published 1998

Published by B T Batsford Ltd,
583 Fulham Road,
London SW6 5BY

Batsford Business Online: www.batsford.com

Printed by
Redwood Books
Trowbridge
Wiltshire

ISBN 0 7134 8377 6

A CIP catalogue record for this book
is available from The British Library

Contents

THE HISTORY OF THE LONDON STOCKMARKET

by Tom Winnifrith

It is 300 years since the first legislation was passed to 'restrain the number of ill practices of brokers and stockjobbers'. During those three centuries what we know as the stockmarket has developed from an almost unregulated arena where gentlemen dealt, from the comfort of a handful of City coffee houses, in a handful of shares to become the third largest stockmarket in the world where shares in almost 3,000 companies worth more than £3,600 billion are traded.

Overseeing the entire transformation has, since 1773, been the London Stock Exchange which, alert to the need to maintain its competitive position, seems set to force the pace of evolution further still as the stockmarket enters its fourth century of regulation.

How it began

The explorer Sebastian Cabot was, in 1553, the first to raise money by offering shares in a joint-stock company. A sum of £6,000 was raised in an offering at £25 a share. The venture prospered as it, accidentally, opened up trade links with Russia (having been seeking a passage to China) and as the Muscovy Company delivered handsome rewards to its initial investors.

Muscovy's success spawned other similar flotations and in 1694 King William III boosted the market by raising £1.2 million through issuing notes in a public offering in order to fund a war with the French. Trading in stocks and shares took place in the coffee houses of London's Change Alley, notably Jonathan's and Garraway's. In the nearby Lloyd's coffee house, insurance brokers conducted their business.

By the late 1760s, 150 brokers had formed a subscription club at Jonathan's coffee house, which continued after Jonathan's moved to Threadneedle Street following a fire. In 1773 the club changed its name to the Stock Exchange. Eighteen years later the foundation stone was laid at the same site in Threadneedle Street in the heart of the City of London which remains the Exchange's headquarters today – although the present 26-storey building dates only from 1972.

The stockmarket and Stock Exchange survived the South Sea Bubble, the Wall Street crash and two world wars relatively unscathed but for the globalisation of financial markets. The growth in the size of the UK stockmarket in the 1960s and 1970s, however, forced dramatic changes.

Hitherto the stockmarket had developed slowly over time. Sometimes it changed of its own accord, as in the way in which more than 20 competing regional exchanges opened up during the 19th and 20th centuries in towns such as Cardiff and Aberdeen but then slowly merged before finally amalgamating into one unit covering the United Kingdom and Ireland in 1973. Similarly, it was the Stock Exchange itself which, in 1908, formalised the distinction between brokers and jobbers. On other occasions, external influences forced the pace – such as the decision to incorporate the Stock Exchange under a Royal Charter, taken on the advice of a Royal Commission set up by Parliament in 1877.

Change in the modern era

One of the early signs of the Stock Exchange entering the modern era was the admission of women to its trading floor in 1973 but many more important changes followed.

The rapid growth in the volumes of stocks being traded on the Stock Exchange meant that traditional settlement systems starting to creak under the strain. Partially computerised in the 1960s, the basic mechanism for checking and passing tickets recording bargains had been unaltered for more than a century. Thus in 1979 the Exchange introduced Talisman, what was then seen as a ground-breaking new computerised clearing system. Talisman's success meant that London maintained its position as the clearing house for all transactions in UK and Irish equities as well as many South African and Australian stocks.

However, trading volumes escalated further with the abolition of exchange controls in 1979. So in 1983 the Exchange put in place the changes which led on 27 October 1986 to what came to be known as Big Bang.

What was Big Bang?

Big Bang encompassed three main changes:

- An end to minimum scales of commission
- An end to the enforced legal separation of jobbers (who dealt

only wholesale in the market) and brokers (who dealt with both the jobbers and with outside investors)
- An end to restrictions on outside ownership of member firms of the Stock Exchange

To support Big Bang, the Stock Exchange introduced SEAQ, a computer-based quotation system for share prices. Market-makers (the old jobbers) entered their bid and offer prices (the prices at which they would buy and sell) individual stocks into SEAQ which would then be displayed on screens in the offices of brokers and investors. Dealers were obliged to deal at their quoted bid and offer price.

Almost overnight the Stock Exchange's famous dealing floor was emptied. But perhaps a more important impact of Big Bang was that it allowed new players to enter the London stockmarket such as the big UK clearing banks, including National Westminster and Barclays and US stockbroking giants such as Salomon Brothers and Merrill Lynch.

In the decade following 1985 annual turnover in UK and Irish equities soared from £105.5 billion to £643.3 billion. Indeed, the competitiveness of the post Big Bang system meant that the UK took business from continental exchanges ('bourses'), reinforcing London's position as the financial capital of Europe.

Change did not stop with Big Bang

The process of change did not stop with Big Bang. Indeed, if anything, it has accelerated over the past decade.

Starting in the mid 1980s, the Stock Exchange realised that in order to maintain its competitive edge it would have to replace the Talisman settlement system with a paperless system of monitoring share trades and ownership. In 1993, the Bank of England (assisted by funding from the private sector) helped to developed the CREST system introduced on a gradual roll-out from mid-1996.

At around the same time, the Stock Exchange altered the terms under which share bargains had to be paid for. Previously, completion had to occur with fixed two week periods known as account periods. Gradually, from 1994, the stockmarket moved to settlement on a rolling basis, firstly within ten working days of execution (T+10) and subsequently to a five-day period (T+5).

Other initiatives continued to flow on a regular basis. Perhaps the most significant was the launch of the Alternative Investment Market on 19 June 1995. Intended to be a successor to the Unlisted Securities Market, AIM was designed to breathe fresh life into the smaller companies sector by providing a less tightly-regulated, and thus cheaper, way to raise capital and gain a public listing. By Christmas 1997, AIM already had more than 300 members.

Outside the regulatory remit of the London Stock Exchange, the even more lightly regulated OFEX dealing arena was also established in 1995.

SETS and order-driven trading

On October 20 1997 the City braced itself for another big bang, the introduction of order-driven trading and SETS – the London Stock Exchange's electronic order book trading system,

By spring 1998 more than 100 of the largest UK equities by market capitalisation were traded on SETS. (As this guide was being written, the Stock Exchange was consulting its member firms about extending to the top 350 companies, the number of equities that are traded on SETS.)

The difference between SETS and market-making is that under

the newer system, any broker wishing to trade a line of shares merely enters the amount of stock and the price at which he is prepared to buy or sell electronically and anonymously into the Stock Exchange's computer. The SETS software then attempts to match buy and sell orders from different brokers. The quoted share value one sees displayed at any one time is the price at which the last trade was transacted.

Because market-makers are no longer needed to put up capital to provide liquidity under SETS, the cost of dealing (in terms of the spread between bid and offer prices) should fall, making London a more cost-effective market to deal in for the investment community. The visibility of the price formation mechanism under SETS also makes it a more attractive system to deal in for those investors whose strategies are based on sophisticated computer programmes.

Though the introduction of SETS was not universally welcomed in London, the change was pushed through as a response to the demands of the global investment community. SETS is only the latest, and will not be the last, of a long line of initiatives taken by the London Stock Exchange so it continues to compete on a world stage.

The future

The London Stock Exchange is already preparing for the great challenges that face European financial markets as they prepare for the next millennium, as well as attempting to seize the opportunities offered to western capital from emerging markets elsewhere in the world.

Although the UK is unlikely to participate in the first wave of countries joining EMU, the Exchange has consulted FTSE 100 members about setting up a parallel order book where equities are quoted in ECUs rather than sterling.

Perhaps more importantly, monetary union is likely to see some rationalisation of the bourses within western Europe. London's high levels of efficiency, cheap dealing costs and the weight of capital behind it give it a significant competitive advantage over its rivals on mainland Europe.

A single European stockmarket could only be a matter of years away. In July 1998, the London Stock Exchange and the Deutsche Bourse in Frankfurt signed a Memorandum of Understanding to form a strategic alliance, with the ultimate aim of developing a joint electronic trading platform to trade one another's stocks and shares. Alliances with other European exchanges are likely to follow.

The London market is also looking to attract business from the developing world. Already, almost a fifth of the equities traded in London are companies based outside the UK. Before Christmas 1997 the Exchange mounted intensive marketing trips to India and China encouraging companies in those counties to follow the trail-blazing example of Beijing Datang Power Generation in seeking to float in on the London stockmarket as the easiest and cheapest way of accessing Western capital.

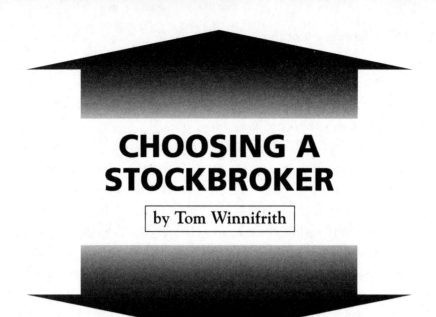

CHOOSING A STOCKBROKER

by Tom Winnifrith

In theory, choosing a stockbroker should be remarkably easy. Surf the Internet for just a few minutes and it will yield almost 100 UK-based firms who desperately want to act for you. For those not on the net, the Association of Private Client Investment Managers and Stockbrokers (APCIMS) will send out a directory of its members in response to a written request. APCIMS is based at 112 Middlesex Street, London, E1 7HY.

In practice, it is the sheer choice of stockbrokers and, more importantly, the variety of services each provide, which can make the act of selection so daunting to a stockmarket novice. Actually, there are really only three types of service offered: execution only, advisory and discretionary.

Execution-only dealing

An execution-only or dealing service is only for those investors who feel certain that they need no advice from their stockbroker and merely want a facility for buying and selling shares. Not surprisingly, the charges for such a no-frills facility are lower than for other forms of stockbroking.

While APCIMS lists around 80 brokers which offer an execution-only service, there are far fewer whose primary focus, and speciality, is – like that of Charles Schwab Europe or of Teletrade – providing a service to the ever-increasing number of ordinary 'Sids' seeking to execute relatively small bargains at the lowest possible cost. Fees for a dealing-only service are normally calculated as a percentage of the size of an individual transaction, but there is likely to be a minimum charge which ranges from less than £10 to more than £20 per trade.

Even the execution-only specialists have, in recent years, started to offer a range of other perks such as telephone hotlines giving share prices, newsletters containing investment advice and market commentary from City professionals or services alerting clients to forthcoming new issues. Most execution-only brokers will also allow clients to trade higher-risk areas than equities, such as the options market.

Ultimately, however, for those seeking an execution-only service, the chief criteria for choosing between various dealing services should be price – which can be ascertained from APCIMS – and the efficacy of dealing and settlement systems, which can be gleaned only from experience.

In the US increasing numbers of investors are using on-line internet-based services to trade shares. Shorn of costly central overheads, such services are increasing competitive pressures within the industry and thus helping to cut dealing costs. In the UK there are a number of small, but rapidly-growing services such as ESI and Infotrade which provide electronic access to dealing systems for as little as £15 or less per bargain.

Advisory dealing

An advisory service is the next step up and, unlike an execution-only facility which can be arranged over the telephone, it is necessary to set up an interview with your prospective broker to establish such a relationship. At a basic level, the professional advises the client on whether to buy, sell or hold individual shares and then – if one wishes to act on that advice – will carry out the appropriate transactions. At a more advanced level, you give your broker full details of your investment portfolio and so, in addition to the basic service, you will also receive regular valuations and advice on your overall portfolio as well as on your position regarding capital gains tax, and how to minimise it.

Almost all brokers providing such a service publish regular newsletters for all their clients reviewing both the whole stockmarket and individual stock selection ideas. Although brokers give you advice on how to invest, no actions can be taken as part of an advisory service without the express consent of the client.

A stockbroker providing an advisory service will offer different suggestions to different clients depending on his understanding of their needs. For instance, while he may suggest that those seeking capital growth buy shares in computer stocks, which pay minimal dividends but are expanding profits rapidly, other clients who need regular income will be steered towards shares in the utilities whose main attraction is the high yield.

Size is important to brokers offering an advisory service. Some advisory services are available only to those with a portfolio worth at least £500,000 but other professionals will handle funds worth as little as £20,000 – a few will even accommodate portfolios valued at just £10,000. Typically, brokers will charge an annual fee of around 1 per cent for managing an investment portfolio and a transaction fee of 0.75 per cent and upwards. Some which charge a higher transaction fee, charge less – or possibly nothing – to administer and vice versa, so it pays to check around to see which fee structure will be most cost effective for you – are you by nature a 'trader' or a long-term investor?

Although one of the bigger City stockbroking names might appear to offer a more cost-effective service, that might not necessarily be the most advantageous selection for all investors. It might be argued that a smaller broker, handling fewer funds, might pay more attention and give 'hotter' tips to the needs of individual clients, especially if the value of their portfolio is at the lower end of the size spectrum. A relationship based on trust is essential to the maintenance of an advisory service and some investors might find that simpler to establish with a local stockbroker. Others will prefer to stick with the security offered by a nationally-known firm, however remote their offices.

Clients of a broker providing an advisory-based service are likely to receive regular calls from their individual advisor and he or she will be easy for you to contact by telephone. Investors are also likely to receive regular written research and market commentaries and, in some cases, invitations to presentations, receptions and seminars hosted by the brokers.

Discretionary stockbroking

A discretionary service is only for those prepared to abdicate the entire responsibility for making investment decisions to their stockbroker. Once you have placed your funds in the hands of a broker providing such a service, he does not need your permission to buy or sell investments – as such it is well-suited to those who have either insufficient time or insufficient knowledge to invest with any degree of confidence.

Although trusting your funds to a discretionary service sounds dramatic, it does not imply a complete loss of control. Before committing any funds to the market, your broker will establish what your investment goals are (mainly in the trade-off between income generation and capital growth) and – depending on your financial circumstances – what sort of risk profile your portfolio should adopt. He or she will also ascertain whether you have any ethical objections to certain types of investments, such as tobacco companies or armaments manufacturers.

A good broker will also provide regular updates on where your money is invested, how your investments are performing and the basic assumptions behind his or her dividend strategy. It is also possible to specify to a prospective broker that certain stocks within your portfolio may not be sold because you believe that they hold great long-term potential.

The charges for a basic discretionary fund are likely to be around 1 per cent of the funds under management and will again vary quite considerably from broker to broker – so it pays to shop around. Most discretionary services require assets of £20,000 although some brokers will go lower.

While only those prepared to cede control of the day-to-day management of their wealth should consider plumping for a discretionary service, it does offer a number of advantages over other types of stockbroker/client relationships.

Perhaps the greatest of these is speed. City professionals are likely to hear of stockmarket developments and rumours minutes, if not hours or days, before ordinary investors and, within the framework of a discretionary service, can act on their superior information to your advantage. By the time a client within an advisory service has been consulted about an investment possibility, that opportunity may already be discounted in the share price.

Another advantage of a full discretionary service is that the broker can handle tiresome and, for many of us, rather confusing, administrative problems associated with share ownership such as the collection and tax treatment of dividend payments.

One point worth checking on a portfolio management service is whether a service is 'closed', in that it invests only in its own funds rather than also investing in products offered by other fund managers. It is also worth checking whether discretionary asset managers are able and have the expertise to invest your wealth in assets other than plain equities or unit and investment trusts. Some of the bigger names in global asset management are well placed to put your cash into more exotic investments such as commodities, traded options, Kruggerands and other metals. Obviously, the fund manager would need clients' prior permission to consider pursuing such higher-risk strategies when he or she considered the timing to be appropriate.

Other services from your stockbroker

When choosing with whom to do business, remember stockbrokers can and will do more than just buy or sell shares for you, and can provide a range of services to help you manage your savings. Indeed, some people are drawn to using the investment services of a particular market professional as an add-on to the other facilities on offer.

Right at the other end of the business spectrum from the large execution-only stockbrokers – whose sole business is dealing in shares – are those who might also offer advice on the placing of cash deposits, TESSAs, ISAs and PEPs, retirement planning,

National Savings, Inheritance Tax and other financial aspects of making a will, school fees schemes, life assurance and mortgages.

Making your final choice

Even if you know for certain what sort of service you want – and from what sort of firm – there are still likely to be at least a dozen candidates in your own imaginary beauty parade. Selecting an execution-only broker is, for most of us who wish to trade only in mainstream shares, largely a function of cost, so that process is relatively scientific compared to picking someone to handle an advisory or discretionary account.

The fees charged by different advisory or discretionary brokers should not be ignored – after all every extra penny of costs is a penny of your profits. More important, however, is the quality of advice and investment decisions provided. Although past performance is no guarantee of future success, it is worth asking not only the firm you wish to use, but also the individual who may be looking after your portfolio, to provide some evidence that they have a track record worthy of respect.

You can check that a firm is properly authorised and regulated by ringing up the Financial Services Authority's Central Register (tel 0171-929 3652). This will tell you what business a firm is authorised to conduct, and whether it is authorised to handle clients' money. Do not be deterred from using smaller firms because of worries about their financial viability. In this industry, as in all others, companies will go bust from time to time. But increasingly strict regulation means that shock collapses are likely to become ever rarer. In addition, all stockbrokers are part of the Investors' Compensation Scheme which ensures that up to £48,000 of an investor's money is protected in the event of a firm going out of business.

When selecting a portfolio management service, the bottom line must be trust in both the integrity and the judgement of the professional adviser. Once you have found a broker you trust and get on with, you could be at the start of a relationship that lasts for decades.

WHAT MOVES A SHARE?

by Tom Winnifrith

A host of factors can decide whether a share price can go up or down, and investors can keep track of them through an ever-increasing range of information sources

In 1815, the Rothschild family was reputed to have made its fortune on the stockmarket because they discovered the result of the Battle of Waterloo days before anyone else. The flow of information has always been the key to predicting share price movements. These days an array of data providers means that all of us – not just the privileged few – can trade in stocks and shares on a relatively level playing field.

Never before has the general public been able to obtain so much information, so easily, about companies quoted on the London Stock Exchange. That is just as well because share prices can move very quickly – and in either direction.

Whether a share is traded on SETS, by a market-maker or on a matched bargain basis, the underlying determinant of its price is supply and demand. If there are more buyers than sellers, a share price will rise and vice versa, whatever system the share is traded on. And the demand for most shares is determined largely by the company's prospects for growing its earnings.

Corporate profits

Share valuation is based on looking forward to future profits rather than back to past performance. That is because in buying an equity one is in effect purchasing a stream of future income in the form of corporate earnings which are either reinvested in the company or returned to shareholders as dividends.

The greater the anticipated growth in future earnings – and thus eventually in dividends – the more investors are typically prepared to pay for an individual share. Consequently, while the average prospective price/earnings ratio for shares in the FTSE All-Share Index is around 18 (meaning that the share price stands at 18 times the earnings per share), most technology and software stocks trade on a forward price/earnings ratio of more than 35 because they are expected to deliver far greater profits growth than the rest of the market.

A lower-than-average price/earnings (p/e) can mean tell the opposite story. For example, say average earnings growth among quoted UK stocks are expected to be around 12 per cent over the coming year. Thus, if a company's shares are valued at less than the average p/e for the All-Share index, the implication is that the stockmarket as a whole expects that company to grow its earnings by less than 12 per cent.

Company announcements

At least twice a year quoted companies must announce their results via the Stock Exchange. Increasingly, companies will also issue trading statements just before the end of their financial year (or at other times if business has been far better, or more usually far worse, than most analysts expect) in order to prevent unnecessarily sharp movements in the share price.

In days gone by, market expectations were 'massaged' through informal briefings from the company via its corporate adviser or broker to the wider investment community. Information that could potentially affect the price of a share is known as price-sensitive information. Tighter legal guidelines and increasingly rigorous monitoring of insider-dealing legislation by the Stock Exchange mean that nowadays any price sensitive news must be distributed to the market via an official announcement on the LSE's Regulatory News Service (RNS).

Between formal announcements from companies, large stockbrokers employ analysts with expert knowledge of individual sectors, to predict corporate profits and, based on those forecasts, to advise whether the shares are overvalued or cheap. At any one stage there are likely to be around two dozen analysts in London covering the larger FTSE 100 stocks and their in-depth knowledge of the companies they cover and of trends in each industry generally ensure that the financial community has a reasonable idea of how the country's largest companies are performing.

However, many smaller companies on both the full list and the secondary AIM market are unlikely to be followed in such depth. A less extensive research base means that the potential for surprises, both pleasant and nasty, at results time is all the greater. That, in turn, is likely to cause greater volatility in the share price.

The tightening of regulation concerning insider dealing means that investors are most likely to receive information which may cause a change in expectations about profits at the time of annual and interim results, the chairman's speech at an annual meeting and intermittent trading statements. Companies normally publish formal notification of the dates of results and their AGM so investors can brace themselves for an effect on the share price.

Other influences inside the company

It is not just results that must be posted via the RNS system but any announcement that the company and its advisers believe is likely to be 'price sensitive'. Thus news of all acquisitions, fund raisings and boardroom changes, and significant purchases or disposals of shares must be notified to the investment community via the Stock Exchange.

The sudden and unexpected departure of a key director can, in some cases, cause a sharp fall in a company's share price if analysts fear that it may be a sign of trading difficulties or boardroom disagreements about the company's future direction. In itself the departure may be meaningless but if it causes investors to query their expectations of future earnings growth, the shares will be sold down to a lower price.

Likewise, what a director does with their shares is also of interest to the investment community, and all director dealings must be notified to the market.

A company may also be forced to issue a formal statement in response to a sharp rise in its share price, either because of advice from its professional advisers or because the Stock Exchange orders it to do so to prevent the creation of a disorderly market in its shares. A sharp rise in a company's share price often prompts a statement informing the market that the company has received a bid approach.

Companies must also signal when they are paying dividends. The shares will then be flagged as ex-dividend when payments are assigned to investors. On the day that the shares 'go ex' one would expect to see the headline share price fall by the value of the dividend payment.

Outside influences

Sometimes a company's share price will move sharply because of events entirely outside its control. Shares are heavily influenced by the performance of companies in the same sector. A profits warning from one company can sees shares in its competitor also fall – or rise if the rival company is seen as a stronger player gaining market share.

Share prices will also be moved on the back of research notes published outside the results season by leading analysts. Not every broker has the power to 'move markets' but those pundits who have established a reputation for calling stock selection accurately over many years will trigger sharp movements in individual share prices merely by changing their recommendation on a particular stock. If men such as NatWest Securities oil analyst Fergus MacLeod or CSFB's pharmaceuticals guru Steve Plag predict that a company's profits will fall, their track record of accuracy suggests the profits will indeed fall and the stockmarket revises its expectations accordingly.

Keeping abreast of share prices

For those working in the City, it is almost impossible not to be aware of the latest share prices. In offices around the City, investors can gain up-to-the-minute information from a range of screen-based systems, mainly those provided by ICV's TOPIC system, Reuters or Bloomberg as well as from unique products developed in-house by various broking firms.

Outside the City, gaining information has traditionally been rather tougher but is now becoming easier by the day. Most companies have their share prices displayed in the *Financial Times*, and a majority in *The Times* and *Daily Telegraph*, but even the FT service is not fully comprehensive and all newspaper prices are soon out of date. However, newspaper stockmarket reports can at least be relied on to provide a fairly comprehensive summary of the most significant changes in analysts' stock recommendations.

Most broadsheet newspapers offer a real-time telephone share price information service at a cost of up to 50 pence a minute.

For the investor interested only in larger company shares, BBC 2 and Channel 4's Teletext services provide an almost real-time coverage of most of the shares in larger quoted companies together with a CEEFAX news service. Share prices are updated every 20 minutes.

Up to date information is more expensive

Those not averse to running up a phone bill might also consider using the share price information services provided by a plethora of private client stockbrokers. These may include real-time prices, stockmarket reports and the latest announcements from a company. Many also include broker's recommendations so you can ring up and find out whether a particular stock is considered a buy, a sell or a hold.

However, it is the Internet revolution which has really narrowed the information gap between private client investors and the City professionals. The cost of services varies widely, but anyone with access to the net can access not only real-time share price providers ranging from newspaper-originated services such as the FT to specialist internet players such as Market-Eye.

And internet services such as Market-Eye offer so much more for private investors than mere equity prices. Most offer data about quoted companies trading record and balance sheet history while some also offer fairly comprehensive charting facilities for those who believe that the pattern of a share price graph holds some clues to the future direction of the share price. Other packages, such as Investor 2, download data from Teletext to offer share price information, charting services and packages utilising the basic tools of investment analysis.

Most quoted companies now have their own Internet homepage allowing the private investor immediate access to the company's recent press releases and annual reports as well as a stack of rather less useful information.

Meanwhile, specialist information providers such as The Estimates Directory (which offers a list of brokers profit and dividend forecasts and investment recommendations for most UK traded equities) and Company REFS have in recent years started offering an Internet-based alternative to their printed products.

An easy entree into all of the opportunities offered by the Internet is InvestorLinks (www.investorlinks.com) a page that contains literally thousands of links into other websites providing information for the investment community.

..and a good stockbroker is invaluable

Ultimately however, all such media forms only transmit, at best, second-hand information to the private investor. There is no substitute for gaining access to someone who has direct exposure to the very latest developments and rumours at the centre of the financial markets. Execution-only stockbrokers may appear cheaper than those offering an advisory service but the latter should be abreast of stock recommendation changes by leading analysts, of RNS announcements and of the latest rumours doing the rounds.

The more closely one needs to track a share price, the more expensive it becomes. But in an era when the speed of electronic trading can mean an investment loses half its value in minutes, short-term cost-cutting can eventually prove an unaffordable luxury.

INVESTMENT CLUBS

by Juliet Oxborrow

Investing in shares requires capital and know-how. You may have
a little of each but not enough to run a successful and properly
diversified portfolio. One option, in this case, is to invest in a
collective fund such as unit trust. This will allow you to tap into
the fortunes of dozens of shares, but as far as taking investment
decisions is concerned you are taken out of the equation
completely. All the decisions as to what shares to buy and sell
are taken by the fund manager, and you'll only find out about
them after the event in a half-yearly report.

But there is another way to pool resources and have a hand in
the running of your portfolio – start an investment club. All you
need is a group of interested friends and enough cash to make a
regular contribution. It won't obviate the need to arrange a
pension and other proper financial planning, but an investment
club can be a lot of fun and you'll have the satisfaction of
knowing that any profits you make are down to your own hard

work. Another encouragement is that investment clubs regularly outperform professional fund managers.

Background to investment clubs

Investment clubs, unsurprisingly, began life in that hotbed of entrepreneurship, the United States. The first recorded club started life in 1898, in Texas, but the main force behind the movement was Frederick Russell, who formed an investment club in the mid-1940s to provide capital to start up a small business. Russell died in 1965 but his club, the Mutual Investment Club of Detroit, has kept on going. Since its formation, club members have contributed a total of US$426,000, and their portfolio and withdrawals total US$5 million.

America is now home to 37,000 investment clubs, with 730,000 members between them. The UK got in on the act in the late 1950s, and British investment clubs have enjoyed a new prominence since ProShare, the not-for-profit organisation which promotes share-ownership, acquired the National Association of Investment Clubs in 1993. Currently, there are more than 2,000 clubs affiliated to ProShare, with over 25,000 members signed up.

Starting your own club

Investment clubs can be run on a casual basis but to run a club properly you should get hold of the ProShare manual, costing £25. This explains the steps to take to set up a club and how to ensure its smooth and efficient operation, including selecting a stockbroker and what computer software to use.

You should also become a member of ProShare Investment Clubs, although there is no obligation to do so. Full membership of

PIC is free for the first year and costs £25 per club thereafter. Members get a regular newsletter, access to preferential broker dealing rates, a free copy of *Company REFs* (Really Essential Financial Statistics) which provides detailed profiles of more than 2,500 companies, and an opportunity to enter national competitions and the PIC annual awards.

A ProShare-affiliated investment club can have up to 20 members. This allows it to run as a partnership – any more members and it would have to be registered as a limited company, which is more expensive and more complex taxwise.

Members agree to a joining fee and regular minimum subscription, which everyone can easily afford. The typical subscription, says ProShare, is £25-£30 a month per member. Setting an appropriate level of subscription is crucial: if it isn't money that members can afford to lose, portfolio losses can lead to resentment.

Of course, different members may want to contribute more than others and this can be made possible by unitising the portfolio, that is dividing the portfolio's net asset value into units of equal size. As with a unit trust, the units will rise in value as the net asset value increases, and drop if it falls. Each member share is valued at the unit price multiplied by the number of units each holds. Unitisation, which can be handled easily through investment software, allows members to buy more units, or sell them back, reasonably easily, although clubs should be wary of any one member having a disproportionate share. It also means new members can join at a later date with the minimum of complication.

Holding meetings

Members should be willing to commit an evening a month to meeting plus a few more hours to research companies or fulfil other club duties.

Clubs need to elect three members to act as chairman, treasurer and secretary. Minutes should be taken and written up by the club secretary and meetings should follow a fixed agenda, with, for example, the treasurer firstly announcing the latest portfolio valuation, followed by consideration and discussion on the club's portfolio and its expansion.

All investment clubs emphasise the importance of democracy in the stock selection process. All stock purchases and sales should be put to the vote on a one-member, one-vote basis.

Administration and share-dealing

Two key decisions will be which stockbroker to use to buy and sell stocks on the club's behalf and how to register shares. Your club may want to use a stockbroking firm with which a member has already built up a relationship, but there are a number of brokers which offer specific services for investment clubs, including exclusive brokerage rates (see box on page 30).

In order to buy and sell shares, there must be a designated shareholder. As partnerships, investment clubs cannot legally hold shares in their own name. The two most feasible solutions are either to elect two or three club members as trustees and register all shares in their names, or to use a nominee account offered by your chosen stockbroker. Most major stockbrokers offer nominee accounts and strongly advocate their use now that share trades have to be settled in five days. This will cut down on paperwork for the club, as all share certificates will be held by the nominee as the legal shareholder, but clubs must be sure that the nominee manager passes on information concerning dividends, rights issues, shareholder perks, and so on.

Initially, the most off-putting aspect of running a club is the administration – maintaining proper accounts and keeping portfolio valuations up to date. But, says ProShare, if all of these aspects are taken care of with the right investment software from day one, they need only involve a couple of hours' work a month.

Making your club a success

Some investment clubs do flounder early on but with dedication, many more flourish and become an important monthly social event for their members as well as a way of potentially making money. Follow the tips below to make your club a winner.

* Establish at the outset what your investment objectives are and the type of companies you are interested in;
* Hold monthly meetings in one location such as a pub or club;
* Have a fixed day of the month for meetings, and be strict about attendance;
* Make sure each member has an equal amount of input; don't let one member become overbearing;
* Use members' own strengths – some will be good at number-crunching and studying price-earnings ratios, others at keeping an eye out for up-and-coming companies and investment opportunities in the press; and another at writing the club's monthly newsletter;
* Keep meetings business-like but make sure they are relaxed and fun as well;

- Plan social activities for club members, such as company visits and a Christmas dinner with partners;
- Be realistic about returns – and be prepared for no or low returns in the first six to twelve months.

For more information about investment clubs, contact ProShare on tel: 0171-394 5200.

Stockbrokers running special services for investment clubs

Barclays	tel: 0800 551177
Lloyds Stockbrokers	tel: 0345 888200
Charles Shwab	tel: 0121-200 2474
Caterdeal	tel: 01708 738688
NatWest	tel: 0171-895 5000

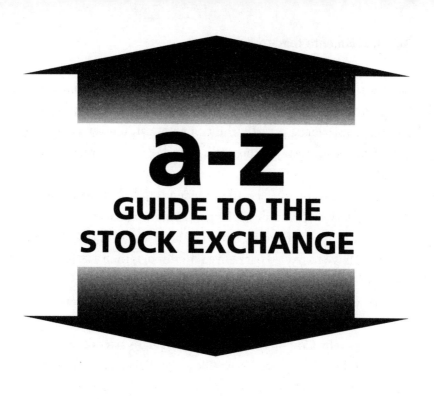

a-z
GUIDE TO THE STOCK EXCHANGE

Accounting Period

The period, usually 12 months, covered by a company's *annual report and accounts**.

Advance Corporation Tax (ACT)

ACT is the system in place until April 1999 by which British companies are taxed on share *dividends**. The tax, payable when a distribution is made to shareholders, is treated as an advance

* denotes a word or words having a separate entry

payment of *Corporation Tax**. If the amount of ACT paid out is higher than a company's total liability to Corporation Tax during a particular *accounting period**, the company can carry forward the excess to set against a future year's tax bill or surrender it to a subsidiary company's tax bill.

The payment of ACT entitles dividends to hold a *tax credit** of 20 per cent, which can be reclaimed by non-taxpayers and PEPs. Basic-rate taxpayers have no further liability to tax but higher-rate taxpayers have to pay 20 per cent more through their tax return to match their rate of 40 per cent.

The system of ACT and tax credits is to be abolished from April 1999, and the government is planning to phase in over four years a system whereby Corporation Tax is paid each quarter on expected profits, although smaller companies can be exempt from this system. This would bring the taxation of UK companies in line with the US.

Advisory dealing service

Investment managers and *stockbrokers** offer three basic types of service to their clients: '*discretionary**', '*execution-only**' and 'advisory'. The first type means that the manager is entirely responsible for the choice of investments, although the client can lay down guidelines at the start (such as not wishing money to be invested in arms companies).

The second type means that the manager merely carries out the client's dealing instructions. The third type allows a continuous dialogue between broker and client.

The extent of an advisory service can vary. The stockbroker will discuss the merits of buying or selling a *share** with the client before dealing, and the discussions will be more or less personalised and detailed depending on elements like how much the stockbroker is charging. Some stockbrokers will contact a client to discuss an investment idea, while others expect clients to contact them when they want advice about an appropriate course of action.

Alternative Investment Market

The Alternative Investment Market, or AIM, opened for business on 19 June 1995 with just 10 companies. Three years on, membership has grown to more than 300.

AIM offers a means for small companies to raise capital and for investors to put money into growing enterprises.

While a full listing on the main market can cost around £1 million in fees to lawyers, PR consultants and so on, an AIM listing can cost as little as £50,000. Companies have to be brought to the market by a 'nominated adviser*'. These advisers are merchant banks and stockbroking companies nominated by the Stock Exchange. The requirements for an AIM listing are less burdensome than those of a full Stock Exchange listing. Many companies float on AIM with the intention of graduating to the main Stock Exchange at a later date.

Private investors can buy shares in AIM companies through stockbrokers, and a number of investment funds specialise in AIM shares. Investment in AIM companies, however, is likely to carry a higher level of risk than investing in larger companies with a full listing on the Stock Exchange.

To encourage investment in young and growing companies, the Inland Revenue offers investors in AIM shares certain tax breaks (in the same way as other unquoted shares) through the *Enterprise Investment Scheme** and *Venture Capital Trusts**.

Furthermore, capital losses from AIM investment can be set

against income tax. It is also possible to get *Capital Gains Tax** relief by reinvesting taxable gains in AIM shares, although since April 1998 this facility has only been available to investment in newly-issued AIM stocks.

Annual general meeting (AGM)

Held for the benefit of shareholders in a company to announce the company results for the last accounting period, to vote on shareholder issues such as new board members and to give the opportunity to shareholders to ask the company to account for its actions. Anyone holding ordinary shares in a company is invited to attend the annual general meeting and vote. Voting can also be carried out by proxy or by post. If you hold shares through a stockbroker's nominee account, you may not be invited to the AGM automatically. So alert your broker if you wish to attend future meetings.

If a voting issue arises between annual meetings, a company can hold an *extraordinary general meeting** (EGM).

Annual report and accounts

Under UK law, a company is required to report to its shareholders on how the business is doing. This is done through the annual report and accounts. Shareholders on a company's register will be sent a copy of the report and accounts each year. Anyone who invests in a certain company, or who is thinking of investing in it, should take the trouble to read them, as they give a good indication of a company's health and future plans.

The standard of company reports varies, with some being more informative and/or glossy than others, but by law all must contain elements such as a chairman's statement, profit and loss account, balance sheet and auditor's report. There are also a number of other elements.

Part of a report and accounts consists of narrative statements. The chairman's statement usually consists of general comments about the company, and may include information about new developments that the company has undertaken in the past year. It should also give some idea about future developments and prospects.

The directors' report deals with the financial activities of the company, including any acquisitions or disposals, and political donations. It should also state how many *shares** and *options** over shares each of the directors holds, and how their holdings have changed during the year. If a significant number of directors have sold shares, investors might treat this as a warning sign, although it may also be that they are taking profits, having exercised share options.

A feature of the report is the operating and financial review, a commentary on the year's activities. After this come pages of figures: the balance sheet, profit and loss account, cashflow statement and financial summary.

The balance sheet balances the company's net assets against shareholders' funds. Assets are divided into fixed assets such as plant and machinery, and current assets such as stock, deposits and monies owed to the company. From these the company has to deduct its current liabilities, such as creditors, overdrafts, *Corporation Tax** and the *dividend** capital that is to be paid out to shareholders. The figure that results should equal the capital that was originally raised by issuing shares, and any profits that have been retained by the company.

The profit and loss account gives several figures including the company's turnover, its profit or loss before tax, and a breakdown of Corporation Tax paid. What is left over after tax is the net profit, and the profit and loss account also shows how much of this has been distributed as dividends to shareholders, and how much profit has been retained by the company.

The cashflow statement shows how much cash has been generated by the business and from other sources, and how much has been spent, for example, on repaying loans or investing in new equipment. The financial summary highlights key figures from previous years, and is useful for comparing the current year's results with those of previous years.

Finally, there is the *auditor's report**. This can be a 'clean' report, meaning that the auditors are happy that the company has given a true and fair view of its financial position, or a 'qualified' report. The latter could indicate problems, or merely that the auditor disagrees with some area of the company's accounting.

APCIMS

The Association of Private Client Investment Managers and Stockbrokers, or APCIMS, is a trade association for stockbroking firms and some fund managers that offer services to private investors. Although its main role is to look after the interests of its members, by extension it also looks after the interests of the public, on whose business these *stockbrokers** and fund managers rely.

APCIMS publishes a national directory of private stockbrokers and the services they offer. It gives details, for example, of whether they offer *advisory dealing** as well as *discretionary** and *execution-only** dealing, the minimum portfolio they accept for discretionary management, and an idea of their dealing and management rates. The directory is available, free of charge, from APCIMS, 112 Middlesex Street, London E1 7HY.

Arbitrage

A technique of transferring funds or goods from one market to another to take advantage of a difference in interest rates, currency exchange rates or commodity prices in order to make a profit. 'Arbitrageurs' can be found on the dealing floors of banks and stockbroking houses.

'At best'/'At limit'

If you instruct your *stockbroker** to buy or sell a particular share 'at best' he or she is obliged to deal in the stock at the best price available on screen at the time your order is placed with a *market-maker**.

Shares are quoted with a spread, so for example if Abbey National shares are quoted at 1171p-1176p. The best price at which you can sell is 1171p and the best buying price is 1176p. Alternatively you can buy 'at limit'. You state a price at which you are willing to buy or sell and the deal is done when a suitable match comes along.

As well as dealing through market-makers, the new *SETS** system of computerised dealing can also accept 'at best' and 'at limit' orders.

Auditor's Report - see *Annual Report & Accounts**

Balance Sheet - see *Annual Report & Accounts**

Bargain - A deal made on the *Stock Exchange**

Basket trade

The purchase of a group of stocks for one price, although they may be recorded individually for accounting purposes.

Bear - see *Bulls & Bears**

Bearer securities

Some *securities** are issued in 'bearer' form, which means that possession of the share or bond certificate denotes ownership of the *share** or *bond**. You are most likely to come across them if you invest in overseas shares outside the UK.

In the UK, ownership of shares and *stocks** is generally recorded centrally in a register of shareholders kept by the issuer. This register enables *dividends**, *rights issues** and so on to be allocated when they occur. Where bearer shares are issued, there is no register of shareholders. Dividends, for example, are claimed by sending in a coupon attached to the share certificate, and the owners of the shares can therefore remain anonymous.

While it is important to look after all share certificates carefully, it is particularly important to look after bearer shares, since there will be no register to prove your right to the shares if the certificates are lost or damaged. Most *stockbrokers** and banks offer safe custody services for share certificates and other documents, and you can choose to keep the certificates in the UK or in the country where they are issued.

If you invest in offshore funds (similar to unit trusts) in locations like Luxembourg, you will often be given the choice of having bearer certificates or registered certificates, since fund managers are accustomed to catering for different investment cultures. One point to be aware of if opting for bearer certificates is that UK fund managers who operate *share exchange** schemes for their *unit trusts** and *investment trusts** may not accept bearer shares in exchange for their funds.

Bears – see *Bulls and Bears**

Bed & Breakfast

Bed & breakfasting used to be a popular technique to reduce future *Capital Gains Tax** (CGT). It involved selling shares one day then buying them back the next to realise a gain or loss. Losses could be realised to set against taxable gains on other assets in order to reduce a current tax bill. Alternatively, by realising gains an investor could reduce future tax liabilities since repurchasing assets creates a higher base price from which future gains are calculated, and it can make use of the current tax year's capital gains allowance.

The March 1998 budget has limited the scope for bed & breakfasting, with Inland Revenue decreeing that sales and repurchases of shares within 30 days will be cancelled out for *Capital Gains Tax** purposes. Investors can hold the shares for just longer than 30 days but then run the risk that the price will move before they buy back the shares.

Benchmark

Any fixed standard by which investment performance is measured. UK fund managers commonly use UK indices such as the FTSE 100 or the FTSE All-Share Index against which to gauge whether they have out, or underperformed or been broadly in line with the market. International funds may use the FTSE World Indices or the MSCI World Index.

Fund managers may also used benchmarks as a rough guide for asset allocation, going underweight, overweight or neutral in a particular share or asset relative to an index's own weighting in a bid to outperform it.

Investors need to be sure they are using a suitable benchmark to contextualise performance. There is little point using the FTSE 100 index as a benchmark for example, if you insist on having 40 per cent on your portfolio in cash deposits.

Best advice

Under the Financial Services Act passed in 1986, financial advisers are obliged to give their clients 'best advice', having first ascertained their details from a thorough fact find. *Independent Financial Advisers** are obliged to recommend from the whole market the most suitable product for a client's needs, while 'tied advisers' can only recommend their company's products if they fit in with the client's requirements. If none is suitable, a tied adviser must say so.

Bid

The price at which a market-maker will buy shares, being the lower of the two figures quoted on *TOPIC** screens under the *SEAQ** system of dealing shares in the UK, the higher price being the *offer price**. The difference between the two prices is known as the *bid/offer spread**. Unit trusts are also subject to a bid and offer price.

Also refers to an attempted takeover of one company by another.

Bid/offer spread

The difference between the prices at which securities such as shares and unit trusts can be bought and sold by investors. The spread provides the *market-maker** or adviser with commission on the deal. Computerised dealing under *SETS**, where no market-maker is involved, is expected to lead to a narrowing, if not the disappearance, of the spread on shares, and some unit trusts which sell direct to the public now trade with no or only a small spread.

Big Bang

The momentous day of 27 October 1986 when the London Stock Exchange under went something of a revolution, as a new system of trading came into action.

Until Big Bang, trading was done in two tiers. There were *jobbers**, also known as market-makers, who stood on raised benches on the floor of the Stock Exchange and made a market in *shares**, setting a price at which they would buy and sell them. They made their money from the 'jobber's turn' – the difference between the buying and selling price of a share.

Rather than selling shares to the public, jobbers sold them to (or bought them from) *stockbrokers**, who traded on the Stock Exchange floor on behalf of their clients and made their money from fixed commissions charged on the deal.

Jobber and stockbroker firms were partnerships and could not be owned by outside companies. This made it difficult to raise large amounts of capital and was preventing them from competing with, for example, Wall Street's large broking firms. But in 1986, Stock Exchange membership rules changed, allowing banks and securities houses, both from the UK and overseas, to own stockbroking firms. The distinction between jobbers and stockbrokers was also abolished, and firms could act in either or both capacities, as they wished. In the run-up to Big Bang, there was a huge shopping spree in the City of London and many long-established stockbrokers were gobbled up by British and American banks.

Since these institutions now had their fingers in many different pies, there were new opportunities for insider dealing, and the new financial giants were required to set up 'Chinese Walls'* to ensure that the fingers of the left hand did not know what the fingers of the right hand were doing, nor in what pie they were doing it.

In order to boost competition in this new financial marketplace, minimum commission rates were abolished.

The other main change was technological, and was the replacement of the Stock Exchange floor by a computer-based price quotations system called Stock Exchange Automated Quotations (SEAQ*). Market-makers* entered their buying and selling prices into the system, which then transmitted them electronically into brokers' offices. Now, instead of a physical dealing floor, trading takes place through the computer or over the telephone.

Black Monday

October 19 1987, the day America's Dow Jones Industrial Average saw the largest fall in its history. A 108-point fall on the Friday, precipitated by disappointing trade figures, rising interest rates and a fall in the value of the dollar, guaranteed panic selling when trading started again on the Monday and, sure enough, the Dow fell a massive 508 points.

The UK responded on the same day with a 249.6 point drop on the FTSE 100. The UK market saw a further 250-point fall on the Tuesday and further falls throughout the week.

Black Tuesday

October 29 1929, the day of the US stockmarket crash ('The Great Crash') which led to the Great Depression of the 1930s, although the date is often pinpointed to the previous day when the Dow Jones Industrial Index fell 13 per cent (the original Black Monday).

Black Wednesday

September 16 1992 – Sterling was pulled out of the Exchange Rate Mechanism and fell instantly from a value against the German Deutschemark of DM2.78 to DM 2.64, leading to calls for the resignation of the then Prime Minister John Major and Chancellor Norman Lamont. While the currency fell, the move out of ERM proved good for investor sentiment and the *FTSE 100 Index** rose 105 points the next day, to 2483.9.

Blue chip

Originating from the highest-value chip in poker, this description applies to the ordinary *shares** of the largest companies on a *stock exchange**.

Major stockmarket indices such as the *FTSE 100** are largely composed of blue chips. Familiar blue chip names are Abbey National, ICI and J Sainsbury.

There is no exact way to define a blue chip company, but a dominant market share, a vast market capitalisation (that is the share price multiplied by the number of shares in issue) and a highly respected name are the usual hallmarks.

A blue chip company is valuable to investors because it tends to offer relatively reliable, steady growth or income, and its share price will rarely go crashing down or shooting through the roof. Because of this stability, blue chips feature heavily in the portfolios of non-active investors who don't have time to keep a close eye on the stockmarket. They are also a mainstay of many institutional investments such as pension funds, which are required to be generally conservative in their choice of investments.

Bonds

Bonds is the term given to all *securities** where the issuer guarantees the repayment of capital at a fixed point in the future. Basically, then, they are a type of IOU with a set repayment date. In the meantime, most bonds pay a fixed rate of interest, although some pay a variable rate (floating rate bonds), others pay a rate linked to the rate of inflation (index-linked), and others pay no interest but give a capital gain (zero coupon bonds).

Issuing bonds is the main way in which governments across the world can raise money for public expenditure. In Britain, bonds issued by the government are known as *gilts**. It is disputed whether this name came about because the bond certificates had a gilt edging or because the credibility of the issuer was great enough that they were 'good as gold'.

In America, the main form of bond is the treasury bill, or T-bill, while there is also a large market in municipal bonds. They are also issued by companies (corporate bonds) and by organisations like the European Investment Bank.

Where bonds are backed by governments of economically developed countries, they are among the least risky investments available. Since it is unlikely, but not impossible, that the issuer will go out of business and be unable to repay the capital, there is virtually no risk of losing your money, particularly from governments like the UK and the US. However, government bonds from less developed countries tend to have a higher risk of default.

The rate of interest on a bond is referred to as the *'coupon**' because once upon a time all bond certificates had coupons which were torn off and presented when the interest payment was due. Most bonds are issued with a fixed rate of interest which is paid twice-yearly. The amount of interest paid is expressed as a percentage of the bond's par value – the price at which the bond is repaid. So if the bond's par value is £100 and the coupon is 5 per cent, you will receive £5 interest a year. Bonds can be short, medium or long-term, and their average life is five to ten years.

Once issued, a bond can be traded on the stockmarket where it may be bought or sold for more or less than its par value. Prices of bonds usually depend on interest rates. For example, a bond paying 5 per cent is likely to trade for less than its par value if the general interest rates rise to 8 per cent. This means that there is some capital risk attached to bonds because prices fluctuate in line with short-term rates and supply and demand.

Income and *Capital Gains Tax** on bonds varies from country to country, and the Eurobond was developed to make bonds more tax-efficient for international investors. Since Eurobonds are not issued in any one country, they can be paid without deduction of tax.

In the UK, income from bonds is liable to income tax, but capital gains are not taxed.

'Bonds' also acts as a blanket description for some of the fixed-term products issued by life assurance companies. This can be slightly confusing because these 'bonds' may invest in all sorts of holdings from equities to property to cash, and the return of capital may not be guaranteed.

Bourse

The French word meaning 'purse', bourse originally referred to the Paris stock exchange but other European exchanges have adopted it as well.

British government stock – see *Gilts**

Broker

Primarily shorthand for *Stockbroker**, but can refer to a range of financial intermediaries including mortgage brokers and insurance brokers.

Broker funds

Pooled investment funds set up by *stockbrokers** and *Independent Financial Advisers** for clients who don't have enough capital to achieve a sufficient level of diversification by holding equities directly. The broker may choose the investments or farm out the investment management to a third-party. Many broker funds take the form of *unit trusts**. When considering a broker fund, investors need to be mindful of the initial and management charges involved and the fund's performance record.

Bulls and Bears

The stockmarket is a fertile source of bizarre terminology, not least in its use of animal terms to describe the behaviour of the dealers who work in it.

The two best-known terms are bears and bulls. A bear is a dealer or investor who believes that prices in a *share** or a certain market are going to fall, and is likely to be selling his or her stock. Bulls, on the other hand, believe that prices are going to rise, and will be buying as fast as they can. By extension, a bull or bullish market is one where prices are rising or expected to rise, and a stale bull is someone who has bought shares in the expectation of a rise in the value, but has not yet seen it and is tired of holding the shares.

Bearish speculators may often 'go short' on a stock, in the belief that its price will fall. This means that should they, for example, have a contract to sell to someone else at a date in the future, rather than building up the stock in question in advance ready for delivery, they will deliberately stay away from the stock, believing they will be able to pick it up more cheaply close to the delivery date. Bullish speculators, on the other hand, may do the opposite and go long, amassing more of the stock than they need, in order to make a profit. Both activities can turn out to be horribly expensive if the speculator misreads the market.

If bears or bulls are present in large numbers on the stockmarket, the effect can be enormous. In a bear market, the general sentiment is that prices are going to fall, and the majority of dealers will be selling as fast as they can to limit their losses. Although external factors may have caused the dealers to take their bearish stance in the first place, the fact that the majority of them are now selling ensures that prices will continue to fall. Similarly, in a bull market, as more and more dealers want to buy shares, demand will drive share prices higher. In both circumstances, a snowball effect can exaggerate movements in either direction.

Nevertheless, there is another type of investor, known as a contrarian, who resists the stampedes of rampant bears and bulls, and invests against the consensus. A contrarian might buy a stock when everyone else is pessimistic about it in the hope that it has reached its base and will rise thereafter.

Also seen stalking the stockmarket from time to time are stags – speculators who buy shares in *new issues** such as *privatisations** in the belief that prices will rise above the issue price immediately, allowing them to sell at a profit when dealing in the shares begins.

Call option

The right, but not the obligation, to buy a stock or share at an agreed price by a certain date in the future. See *Traded Options**.

Capital adequacy

Requirement for firms conducting investment business to have sufficient reserves.

Capital Gains Tax

Tax payable in the UK on appreciation in an asset's value from acquisition to disposal. Capital Gains Tax is payable on any asset, although some everyday items are exempt, including: your main residence, your car, personal possessions with a value of less than (currently) £6,000, wasting assets with a life of no more than 50 years such as yachts, caravans and racehorses, and lottery and betting winnings.

In terms of investment, *Venture Capital Trusts** and the *Enterprise Initiative Scheme** (both within certain limits), *Personal Equity Plans** and *Individual Savings Accounts** can all be used to shield holdings from CGT. National Savings Premium Bonds and Savings Certificates, bonuses from Tax Exempt Special Savings Accounts and SAYE terminal bonuses and particular issues of *gilts** are also not subject to Capital Gains Tax.

Apart from these exclusions, each individual is allowed to make a certain amount of gains each tax year before tax is payable. In 1998/99, this amount is £6,800. There are also a number of devices to reduce tax payable, including deducting the cost of acquiring an item, deducting capital losses on other assets and indexing the acquisition cost in line with inflation so tax is only paid on 'real gains' (although because of changes in the March 1998 budget, costs can now only be indexed as far as April 1998).

In April 1998, the Government also introduced 'tapering' to encourage long-term investment.

This means that the proportion of the gain which is taxable reduces the more years the asset is held. So, in the first three years, 100 per cent of the gain is taxable. After three years, only 95 per cent of the gain is taxable, And this proportion falls by 5 per cent each subsequent year until after 10 years or more only 60 per cent of the gain is taxed.

Business assets are subject to a more generous taper – after 10 years only 25 per cent of the gain is chargeable to Capital Gains Tax.

Cash

One of the three asset classes, along with equities (shares) and fixed interest securities (bonds). Investors use cash as a safe haven – profits from selling investment in equities or bonds may be kept in cash ready to invest again and portfolios may go 'overweight' in cash when stockmarkets are looking jittery. The cash element in an investment portfolio could be an ordinary savings account, a money market account or a money market unit trust which invests across a number of different deposits. Cash will earn interest but over the longer term it does not keep up with the returns from equities nor bonds, which is why it generally constitutes only a small element of a portfolio.

Certificates of Deposit

Issued mostly by merchant banks and discount houses on deposits on typically, between £10,000 and £50,000. The certificate usually entitles the holder to a fixed-rate of interest and is often transferable. CDs can run for periods of three months to five years. CDs are *bearer securities** so whoever holds the certificate is entitled to the interest (whereas a savings account is registered in a particular name).

Certificated sales & purchases

Security transactions where a share certificate is issued and the shares are registered in the purchaser's name. Besides certificated holdings, shares can now be held electronically through *CREST** so no physical share certificate is required.

Chartism

A method of investment analysis which works on the basis that markets follow precise patterns and that future movements in share prices, price/earnings ratios and so on can be predicted by tracking past rises and falls.

Chartism is classified as technical analysis, as opposed to fundamental analysis which hopes to draw conclusions by examining the economic and business environment. Fundamental analysis is used to gauge the long-term prospects for a market or share, whilst technical analysis tends to be used to aid short-term tactical decisions to buy or sell.

Chinese Wall

Since *Big Bang**, investment organisations have been obliged to put measures in place to ensure that one department cannot act on privileged information available to another.

For example, the merchant banking arm of an institution might be involved in bringing a company to flotation on the stockmarket. It would contravene the Chinese Wall requirement for those involved to talk to their colleagues in the company's fund management department about the company's market prospects if this information is not available to competitors and investors generally.

Or a company might work as a *market-maker** and a *stockbroker**; without the Chinese Wall, the stockbroker might be influenced to recommend a stock because a fellow market-maker wants to offload it.

Most companies demonstrate a Chinese Wall physically, for example, the fund management arm of a company may be in a different part of the City of London to the stockbroking department.

Churning

The unacceptable practice of buying and selling securities in an investment portfolio simply to generate commission. Reputable brokers will defend themselves against accusations of churning

by providing clients with a written explanation of why they chose to buy or sell a particular security, and may indicate at the outset what level of turnover they expect to see in a portfolio.

There is no right or wrong level of trading in a portfolio, so it is important to discuss thoroughly with a broker, if you are giving them discretionary management, what proportion of your *portfolio** you wish to hold for the long-term and what level of short-term tactical trades you wish to see. If you are concerned about churning, use an advisory rather than a discretionary portfolio management service, so every trade has to be approved by you first.

Closed-end funds

*Collective funds** which have a fixed amount of capital to invest. *Investment trusts** are closed-end funds. There is an initial subscription offer for shares. Once this has finished, no more shares can be issued, but the ones that have can be bought and sold on the stockmarket.

Because there is a fixed amount of stock, the price of shares will go up and down with demand. Therefore, the share's performance can be different from the performance of the underlying assets in the fund.

Conversely, unit trusts are open-end funds – more units can be created whenever investors demand them, or units can be liquidated when investors want to sell. The unit price is therefore not influenced at all by demand but only reflects the value of the underlying assets. OEICS* are also open-ended.

Closed-end funds is also the name given to investment trusts which invest in other investment trusts.

Collective funds

Investment funds* such as *unit trusts** and *investment trusts** which pool investors' money to invest, thereby giving investors greater diversification than they could achieve alone.

Commission

An adviser's or intermediary's take on the investments he or she arranges.

Stockbrokers earn commission on each security they trade, calculated as a percentage of the value of the deal. A typical level is 1.75 per cent for buying and selling shares and 1 per cent for gilts and other fixed-interest securities, although commission levels vary widely. Most brokers levy a minimum commission per trade, say £15, and commission is tapered so the larger the trade the lower the percentage charged. The lowest levels of commission are on *execution-only** share-dealing services.

Packaged investment products like unit trusts, life assurance and pensions pay commission to advisers, usually comprising upfront commission to cover the initial cost of arranging the investment and renewal or trailing commission payable once a year in return for reviewing its progress.

Commission is met out of the investor's contributions. Under a requirement known as 'hard disclosure' product providers and advisers must show clients how much of their investment is to be deducted as commission and what impact this might have on their investment performance.

Some independent financial advisers don't work on commission but prefer to charge a fee based on how much time they spend on a client's case. In this case, any commission they do earn will be rebated to the client. It is also possible to negotiate with advisers a combination of fees and commission.

Many people prefer to pay fees because there is no danger of product recommendations being influenced by the levels of commission paid in different products, and if they are investing a sizeable amount, they can work out cheaper. However, fees can be more costly if a client wishes to spend a lot of time discussing their situation with an adviser and, unlike commission, fees are usually liable to VAT.

Compensation - see *Regulation**

Consideration

The amount to be paid on a securities purchase or sale (number of shares x price) before charges and stamp duty are added on.

Contract note

Statement confirming a trade in a security sent by a *stockbroker**
to a client the day the deal is done. The contract note will include: the date and time the bargain was struck, a date for settlement (this will be five days after the date of the bargain under the current settlement system of *T+5**); a code number for the deal, and the *consideration** (price per share times the number of shares purchased or sold) plus any additional charges such as commission or stamp duty (only payable on purchases).

The contract note is not proof of share ownership – a share certificate will arrive three to four weeks after settlement. However, it is important to hold on to the contract note to provide evidence of a transaction and to calculate *Capital Gains Tax** liabilities.

Convertibles

Convertibles are a type of security midway between a *bond** and a share. Like both, they are issued by companies to raise capital.

Convertibles can be converted, if the owner chooses, into *ordinary shares** by a specific date at a particular conversion rate, e.g. 15 ordinary shares per 100 convertibles. Until then, they pay a predetermined level of income, usually more than an ordinary share from the same company but less than a bond.

Whether or not you should convert will depend on the performance of the company's shares, and whether you would prefer to keep a fixed income or switch to a potentially more rewarding, but also more risky, asset.

Before conversion, convertibles tend to give some of the best of both worlds. They usually rise in price when shares are performing well, because then the option of exchanging them becomes more valuable. When shares are depressed, they tend to be more resilient because they provide a fixed income and guaranteed capital value at maturity. However, once the right to convert is lost, the bond will become a conventional dated corporate bond, and can experience a sharp price drop.

There are a few specialist *unit trusts** and *investment trusts** investing in convertibles. If you invest in convertibles via a fund, the fund manager will make the decision on whether to convert into ordinary shares.

Some issues of *gilt** are classed as convertibles, offering investors the option of a new gilt holding rather than repayment of capital on maturity.

Corporate bond - see *Bonds**

Corporate governance

The system in place within a company to ensure that it is run in the best interests of shareholders and employees. Corporate governance embraces issues such as directors' pay, pension schemes and how the company books are audited.

In 1998 the Hampel Committee, chaired by Sir Ronald Hampel, proposed a 'Combined Code' setting out principles of good governance and code of best practice. Proposals include a requirement that a company board have three directors who are wholly independent, and for companies to disclose in their *annual report** how they have applied the principles of good governance. Companies' compliance with rules of corporate governance is monitored by the London Stock Exchange.

*Investment trusts** are subject to special rules regarding corporate governance in order to keep trust boards independent from the fund manager. This is to ensure that the trust is run in the best interests of shareholders, not to maximise the fund management company's profits.

Corporation tax

Payable by companies on their trading profits, gains and income. Corporation tax is charged, in 1998/99, at a rate of 31 per cent. There is a small companies rate, payable if a company's profits are less than £300,000, of 21 per cent. The rate increases incrementally until a company's profits reach £1.5 million, at which point it pays the full rate.

Corporation tax is currently paid in two parts in the UK: *Advance Corporation Tax (ACT)** levied on dividends and other distributions to shareholders, and mainstream corporation tax. However, this system is to change from April 1999 and tax will be paid by companies in quarterly instalments, based on expected profits. Smaller companies whose cashflow may not be able to cope will, initially at least, be exempt from the new system.

Coupon

Originally the tear-off part of a bond certificate which, on presentation, entitled the holder to a dividend payment. A bond certificate would be issued with enough coupons to cover each year of the bond's life. Now reference to the coupon simply means the rate of interest payable on a bond, e.g. a bond issued at £100 paying a dividend of £10 has a coupon of 10 per cent.

Crashes

The stockmarket has its ups and downs, but just occasionally there is a sharp fall in the value of *shares**, often as a result of hysteria and panic. The two major crashes of this century have been the Wall Street Crash of October 1929 and *Black Monday** of October 1987. (Market strategists frequently come up with new theories about what makes the stockmarket so vulnerable in that month.)

In addition, there have been periods of protracted declines, such as the bear market of the early 1970s when, as a result of a number of factors including the oil crisis and labour disputes, the *FTSE 30 Index** of the UK's 30 largest companies fell from 543 points in May 1972 to 149 in early 1975.

The crashes of 1929 and 1987 both followed long bull markets and periods of intense speculation, with investors often borrowing money to put into shares that they thought could not fail to go up in value. On both occasions, when the bubble of optimism burst, the results were catastrophic. The Wall Street Crash saw 11 people throw themselves out of windows in Wall Street on a single day, and led to the Great Depression of the 1930s. Black Monday saw 13 per cent wiped off the value of the UK's top 100 companies in a single day, with further losses in the days and weeks that followed. Moreover, it was not just an event confined to the UK, and actually started on Wall Street. The Hong Kong stockmarket was so badly hit that it was closed for a week afterwards.

In both crashes, private investors were badly affected, because following the bull markets of the previous years, many had bought shares for the first time just before the crash without considering the risk attached. Market timing will always be a problem for the private investor who does not have access to the same real-time information as the City, and who cannot react as quickly to market events. One way to avoid this problem is to invest via the regular savings schemes attached to unit trusts* and investment trusts*, which reduce the impact of short-term falls in the markets.

While there are always risks of markets falling, investors should remember that in any ten-year period, the stockmarket has outperformed any other kind of investment.

Credit rating

When companies issue debt such as bonds*, the issues are rated by independent credit-rating agencies, of which the best known are Moody's and Standard & Poor's.

The ratings enable international investors to judge the risk of buying a particular bond. The credit rating assesses the issuer's willingness and ability to make regular interest payments and repay the capital at maturity. The ratings are not a reflection of market risk or prospects for bonds markets. Credit ratings can be upgraded and downgraded as the issuer's circumstances change.

The highest rating possible is AAA at S&P and Aaa at Moody's, and they continue down to D. Anything with a rating of below BB at S&P and Ba at Moody's is speculative.

S&P	Moody's	Comment
AAA	Aaa	Highest rating awarded. Extremely strong ability to service debt
AA	Aa	High quality bonds. Very strong ability to service debt.
A	A	Strong capacity to service debt although more vulnerable to changes in circumstance
BBB	Baa	Adequate capacity to service debt and adequate protection, but more susceptible to circumstances that affect these measures.
BB	Ba	The least speculative within the sub-investment-grade category, although the outlook is uncertain
B	B	Very vulnerable to default, although still able to service debt
CCC	Caa	A real risk of default if financial and economic conditions deteriorate, or possibly even in default (with Moody's)

CREST

The computerised system of share settlement introduced in 1996 to meet the demands of five-day share settlement. Under CREST, shares are registered electronically and there is no need for physical share certificates nor *transfer forms**, although investors can still request a certificate on purchase. CREST does not obviate the need for a *contract note**.

Cum

From the Latin word meaning 'with', to be found in share price listings to indicate that the holder of a security is entitled to a forthcoming capitalisation issue, rights issue or dividend payment, e.g. cum cap, cum rights, cum dividend. See also *'ex**'.

Cyclical stocks

Some types of companies react to economic cycles more strongly than others, falling faster or further in an economic downturn and giving a stronger performance during periods of economic recovery and growth. Because they are so closely linked to the economic cycle, these *shares** are called cyclical stocks and tend to include building and property companies, and companies manufacturing or retailing consumer durables, or luxury goods.

While the principle of cyclical stocks is simple, investing in them is tricky because it involves second-guessing the market. For example, during a period of growth, the share price of a cyclical stock may fall, giving a sign that the growth is reaching its zenith before slowing down or stopping. But because many people are watching the price of that cyclical to get warning of a downturn, and because share prices are determined by market sentiment, there is plenty of scope for false alarms.

Daily Official List

Register of securities listed on the *London Stock Exchange**, produced by Extel, giving the prices at they were traded the previous day.

Debenture

A debenture is a loan secured on specific assets owned by a company. Debenture stock is split into units of £100 and traded on the stockmarket. They are the first loans, after trade creditors, to be repaid if a company runs into difficulties. Because of this, and because they are secured on specified tangible assets, they involve very little risk to the investor. They are usually issued by companies with sizeable assets, such as hotel groups and breweries. Because the risk involved is minimal, debentures are not given *credit ratings**.

Debentures usually have a fixed rate of interest and a fixed maturity date. Because of the low risk involved, the interest rate may be lower than that paid on unsecured stocks that come lower down in the pecking order to be paid. There is unlikely to be much fluctuation in price, although if you buy the stock above par (i.e. above the £100 unit price), you will make a small capital loss when the debenture is redeemed.

Defensive stocks

The *shares** of companies that do not suffer greatly during recessions and economic downturns are known as defensive stocks. The classic examples of this type of stock are food manufacturers, food retailers and utility companies, because people still have to buy food and use electricity and water whatever the economic climate.

A good time to buy a defensive stock is just before the start of a *bear** market or downturn, but it is a sensible idea for a portfolio of shares to contain some defensive stocks at all times because they provide some protection against stockmarket movements. They are also a good balance to less stable types of shares, such as *cyclical stocks**.

Deferred shares

A rare class of *share**, on which the shareholder's right to a *dividend** is deferred until a future date. This may be at a set date, or it may be when the company or its profits reach a certain size. Until that time, the price of the shares is likely to be lower than that of the ordinary shares, rising to the same level as the entitlement comes into effect.

Occasionally, other rights or benefits, such as voting rights, may be deferred until a date in the future.

Demutualisation

The transition from being a financial organisation owned and run solely for the benefit of members to a public limited company owned by its shareholders, who are not necessarily the people who use its services. The first major demutualisation in the UK was the conversion of Abbey National Building Society to a bank in 1989. A further spate of building society demutualisations took place in 1997, when the Halifax, Woolwich, Alliance & Leicester and Northern Rock building societies came to the stockmarket. The Norwich Union life assurance company also chose that year to demutualise, and more conversions among large life companies are expected.

Demutualisation has created a lot of debate in the press, with critics arguing that once organisations have converted to public companies they are run primarily to create profit for shareholders, not to benefit customers. Advocates claim that because public companies are accountable to shareholders they are better run and have greater freedom for expansion.

Members, who must be in majority agreement before an institution can convert, have the added incentive of acquiring shares in the new company at no or low cost.

Derivatives

Derivatives are investment instruments such as *futures** and *options** whose value depends on the price movements of an underlying investment such as a *share**, *bond**, commodity or currency. (Hence they are 'derived' from these underlying investments). They can also be based on financial measurements such as *share indices** and interest rates.

Depending on how they are structured, derivatives can be highly-geared investments, and any rise or fall in the underlying investment can magnify the profit or loss that is made – a feature which is both their attraction and their downside. It has become clear from episodes like the Barings collapse that they can present a huge threat to financial and other institutions because of the enormous losses than can arise from using them.

However, derivatives can also be used to reduce risk; by arranging derivative contracts which rise in value if a market falls, investors can create a hedge against losses. Professional help is needed to do this but there are many packaged products which use derivatives to protect investors' original capital.

Derivatives can be traded on recognised markets like the London International Financial Futures Exchange *(LIFFE*)*, or over-the-counter between different companies.

Designated account – see *Nominee account**

Discretionary dealing

Of all the investment management and dealing services offered by *stockbrokers**, the discretionary service is the most comprehensive. Having worked out with the client what he or she wants, for example, steady growth, low-risk, or no tobacco companies, the investment manager makes all further decisions about the portfolio. Clients are then sent quarterly or half-yearly reports on the transactions carried out, the charges levied and the value of the portfolio.

Some investment managers offer discretionary dealing services for portfolios of as little as £5,000, but it is unlikely that any direct equities will be put into the portfolio unless it is worth £50,000 or more. Below that your money is likely to go into *unit trusts** and *investment trusts**.

Most discretionary managers charge an annual management fee, usually a percentage of the portfolio under management.

Because discretionary management involves handing over the cash and giving a great degree of control to the manager, it is essential to choose one who is authorised to conduct this type of business, and who is trustworthy and competent. The Association of Private Client Investment Managers and Stockbrokers (APCIMS*) publishes a directory of stockbrokers who offer private client services, and this is a good place to start looking for a manager.

Before engaging a discretionary manager, it is important to meet the person who will actually be managing the money (not just the director in charge) and talk with them to see whether the relationship will work. (See also *Advisory dealing** and *Execution-only**.)

Dividends

Returns from shares come in two forms: capital growth from rises in the share price and income, paid in the form of the company dividend.

A dividend is a cut of a company's annual profits, and is usually paid half-yearly.

How much a company decides to pay out as dividends will vary. A young company which needs money to expand might pay out small dividends, or none at all. However, shareholders will expect to be rewarded instead by the share price rising as the company grows. A more established company whose share price is more constant might offer larger dividends to compensate investors for not making large capital gains. Investors have to decide whether they would prefer income in the form of dividends, or wait to achieve a capital gain when the share price increases.

As a general rule, UK companies are a source of higher

dividends than overseas companies, and are therefore valuable for income investors. In the UK, cutting or waiving dividends arouses great ire, while in other investment cultures it may be viewed with more equanimity. The most useful way of looking at dividends and how much is paid out by different companies is to look at the dividend *yield**, which expresses the dividend as a percentage of the share's current market price or its issue price. So if a share is worth £1.20 and the dividend is 10p, the dividend yield is 8.3 per cent, which would be fairly high.

You can see the dividend yields of different companies alongside their share price in the London Share Service section of the *Financial Times*. Bear in mind, however, that this only shows a share's historic dividend yield and is calculated using the dividend that was stated in the company's last *annual report and accounts**; it is not necessarily a reliable guide to what dividend you can expect to receive in the future, although financial commentators will make estimates about a company's prospective yield.

If the report and accounts has only recently been published, new shareholders may still be able to receive the dividend. In that case the share price in the FT will be marked cum-d (cum-dividend). If the time to receive payment has passed, the share price will be marked x-d (ex-dividend).

Until April 1999, UK dividends are paid net of 20 per cent tax, and the cheque should be accompanied by a 20 per cent tax credit which can be reclaimed by non-taxpayers and *Personal Equity Plans**. However, due to changes on the system of *Advance Corporation Tax**, non-taxpayers will no longer be able to reclaim the tax credit and PEPs will receive a notional credit of 10 per cent until April 2004.

Dow Jones Industrial Average

Stockmarket *index** of the 30 largest companies listed on the New York Stock Exchange. It has been compiled by Dow Jones & Co since 1884 (when it only covered 11 stocks). The index was rebased at 100 points in 1928. It hit its lowest point four years later on 2 July 1932 when it hit 41. By mid-1998, it was trading at over 9,000 points. Dow Jones compiles another three indices, following prices in US home bonds, transport stocks and utilities. (See also *Standard & Poor's**, *NASDAQ** and *Russell 2000**.)

The 30 industrial stocks, 20 transportation stocks and 15 utility stocks are averaged at the end of each trading day to create the Dow Jones 'Average', or Dow Jones 'Composite'.

Dual capacity

The system of share-dealing created by *Big Bang**, whereby stockbrokers can both act on behalf of clients and make a market in shares. Previous to this, London was a single-capacity market – brokers had to buy shares through a market-maker or 'jobber', who in turn were not allowed to deal with the public direct.

Earnings per share (EPS)

One of the measurements used by analysts and fund managers when looking at a company's financial health is its earnings per share (eps).

Basically, the earnings per share is the company's profits attributable to shareholders after tax and other expenses have been deducted, divided by the number of shares in issue.

Companies give the latest earnings per share in their annual report. Looking at the growth in a company's earnings per share can be a more enlightening exercise than merely looking at any growth in profits, because the latter figure can be distorted by events like takeovers. Moreover, growth in a company's profits may be diluted if it has issued new shares.

The earnings per share figure is also important because it is used to calculate the company's *price/earnings ratio**, an even more useful indicator when assessing the desirability of a company's shares.

Like all measurements and statistics of this nature, earnings per share figures are most useful when considered in conjunction with the facts behind the numbers. So, for example, if a company's earnings per share have diminished since the previous year, it is worth finding out why, and if that decline looks set to continue, rather than simply dismissing the company out of hand.

Emerging market

An economy that is new to capitalism and share ownership. Emerging markets such as the young markets of the Far East, Latin America and parts of Eastern Europe are attractive to investors because they have massive potential for growth. However they can also be illiquid because there are not enough shares in issue. Also, reliable company information can be hard to come by because companies are not subject to the same rigorous regulatory requirements as their counterparts in more mature markets.

Investors need to be sure that a stockmarket is underpinned by sound economic fundamentals. The Asian miracle – the rapid industrial growth in the Far East – proved something of a mirage in 1997. Companies had overborrowed to fund their impressive expansion and in 1997 many collapsed unable to repay when banks called in their debts. Stockmarkets in Thailand, Indonesia and Malaysia finished the year 70 per cent lower than they started.

A safer way to access some emerging markets is through established companies which have a market there. Mega-corporations like Coca-Cola, IBM and Colgate Palmolive now derive a substantial part of their revenue from emerging markets. Many corporations are now eagerly looking to tap into the biggest emerging market of all, China.

Employee share ownership

A growing number of employees are being offered a stake in the company they work for via employee share schemes, of which there are a number of types.

The most popular type of scheme is Save As You Earn (SAYE), which must be open to all employees in a company, although a qualifying period of employment can be required, up to a maximum of five years.

Under SAYE, employees save between £5 and £250 a month. The contract can be set up for a period of three, five or seven years (although a seven-year scheme only requires the employee to save for five years). The employee's contributions are deducted by the employer from the payroll and lodged with a bank or building society. The price of the shares under option is fixed at the time they are granted, and can be at a discount of up to 20 per cent on the market value.

At the end of the savings period, a tax-free bonus is paid. This bonus is equivalent to three of the employee's monthly payments on a three-year scheme; nine payments on a five-year scheme and 18 payments on a seven-year scheme.

At the end of the savings contract, employees have six months in which to exercise their options. They have three choices:

- close the account and take the payment plus tax-free bonus
- use all the proceeds to take up the option to buy shares
- or taking the proceeds from the account, using just part of them to take up the shares.

Unless the options are exercised early, there is no income tax charge. However there may be a liability to *Capital Gains Tax** if the employee later sells the shares at a profit.

The other main type of scheme is the company share option plan (used to be known as executive or discretionary share option schemes), or CSOP. An employee is granted an option to buy a fixed number of shares at a fixed price in a set period of time. The total value of shares granted to an employee at the option price must not exceed £30,000, and the price of options must not be less than the market value. There is no liability to income tax under a CSOP, provided the options are exercised three to ten years after the options have been granted. More than £30,000 of options can be granted, as unapproved options but will not get the relief from income tax. Again, there is a potential liability to Capital Gains Tax when the shares are disposed of.

Other less common types of scheme are: the long-term incentive plan, which gives an executive a deferred right to receive shares, based on the company meeting a performance target, but provide no income tax relief; convertible share plans, which provide executives in a company with a new type of share which may convert to ordinary shares in the future, depending on set performance criteria; and employee share ownership plans (ESOP), which use a trust structure to distribute existing shares in a company to employees.

Factsheets on employee share ownership are available from ProShare*.

Enterprise Investment Scheme (EIS)

The Enterprise Investment Scheme (EIS) was introduced in 1994 as a way of encouraging investment in new and growing UK companies.

Under the current EIS rules, up to £150,000 a year can be invested in unquoted* companies, which can include companies listed on AIM*. Companies must have gross assets of no more than £10 million, although this can rise to £11 million once it has raised funds through EIS.

Investors in the scheme enjoy a number of tax breaks. To qualify for the tax breaks, the investment must stay in place for at least five years.

First, income tax relief is available on investments at a rate of 20 per cent. So for every £100 invested, the investor only pays £80. Up to £25,000 of investment made in the first half of a tax year can have tax relief assigned to the previous tax year

Second, there is an exemption from CGT* when the shares are disposed of. Third, there is relief against losses made on disposal. Investors can also defer CGT on other assets indefinitely by investing the proceeds in EIS-qualifying shares.

Some activities exclude companies from EIS. Companies providing finance, leasing, legal and accountancy services are excluded, as are companies involved in property-backed activities such as farming and market gardening, forestry and timber production, property development and operating hotels, guesthouses and nursing homes. Shareholders are permitted to become directors in the company but EIS tax relief is not available to anyone with more than a 30 per cent share in a company.

Equity

A stake in any asset such as property, land or a business, although equities have come to refer most commonly as the *ordinary shares** in a company.

Eurobonds

*Bonds** issued on the *Euromarket** and a highly-popular means among large institutions of raising cash. Eurobonds are *bearer securities**, so whoever holds the bond certificate has the right to the dividend on the bond, which is appealing to investors who want anonymity. Dividends are paid without deduction of tax but tax is payable in the investor's home country.

Eurobonds come in various forms: 'straights' pay a fixed rate and run for between three and eight years; floating rate notes have a variable rate of interest, generally based on the London Interbank Rate (LIBOR) and perpetuals have no fixed life and are never redeemed. Some bonds come with warrants attached, giving the holder the right to buy shares in the issuing company. Eurobonds are not widely open to private investors but are primarily of interest to institutions.

Euromarket

A trading platform for shares, bonds and currencies which are outside the jurisdiction of any particular government. Euro does not signify European (although the market originated there and is unofficially headquartered in London). Instead it has come to refer to investments held in currencies outside their country of origin such as Japanese yen bonds held by a German investor or French francs on deposit in Japan – hence eurocurrency, eurodeposit, euroequity or *eurobonds**.

Ex

As opposed to *cum**, ex indicates that the buyer of a security is not entitled to an upcoming payment of dividends, rights issue etc. Shares become ex-dividend a few weeks before the dividend is distributed, at which point they are marked 'xd' in share price listings in the financial press. When the share goes xd, the price usually falls by an amount equivalent to the dividend.

Execution-only

The basic dealing services offered by *stockbrokers**, execution-only services involve a stockbroker merely carrying out the client's instructions to deal without giving any advice about the deal. It is the cheapest type of service, and has got cheaper as telephone-based sharedealing services compete to offer cut-price dealing. So while stockbrokers traditionally charged around 1.50-2.00 per cent for carrying out a client's instructions to buy and sell *shares**, with a minimum of £15-£30, it is now possible to deal for a flat fee of as little as £2.50.

While execution-only dealing does not involve any advice, many stockbrokers do offer their clients a wealth of company and market information. Investors are also benefitting from the advent of Internet execution-only dealing, which allows them to follow prices as they buy and sell.

Although execution-only services are attractive because they enable private investors to cut their investment costs, they are mainly suitable for investors who are confident and experienced. The guiding hand of an investment manager can be useful for the novice investor.

Exercise price

The pre-determined price at which a *traded option** allows the underlying securities to be bought or sold. Also known as the strike price. The attractiveness of the exercise price will depend on the security's current market price. For example, an exercise price below the current market price is attractive on a call option, which gives you the right to buy the security. Conversely, a higher exercise price is desirable on a put option as it gives you the right to sell the security for more than the current market price.

Extraordinary general meeting

A convening for shareholders in between *annual general meetings** if an expedient issue arises, such as voting for new board members in the wake of a sudden resignation or dismissal or if a takeover or merger is proposed.

Final dividend

The dividend paid by a company at the end of the financial year. Companies usually also pay a smaller interim dividend halfway through the financial year.

Financial Services Act

Passed in 1986, the *Financial Services Act** provided the bedrock for the current system of financial regulation. In particular it put in place a chief regulator, the *Securities & Investments Board (SIB)** and a number of assisting self-regulatory organisations to police different types of business.

The Financial Services Act also introduced the concept of polarisation, creating a clear demarcation between *independent financial advisers** and advisers, or salesman, who are tied to one company and its products.

Finally, the Act introduced compensation for investors if a firm ran into trouble through the *Investors' Compensation Scheme**.

Financial Services Authority (FSA)

When Labour came to power in 1997 it vowed to improve the system of financial regulation to protect investors and consumers. Its first move was to rename the chief regulator the *Securities &*

Investments Board*, calling it instead the Financial Services Authority.

The name reflects the wider remit of the new authority. In particular, it is to take over supervision of banks from the Bank of England, and will also regulate building societies, friendly societies and credit unions. By the end of 1999, it will also have absorbed the three self-regulatory organisations, the *Personal Investment Authority**, the *Securities & Futures Authority** and the *Investment Management Regulatory Organisation**.

Investors can get factsheets about the FSA by contacting 0171-638 1240.

FTSE 100 - see *FTSE Indices**

FTSE indices

The *Financial Times* publishes a number of stockmarket indices by which investors and the city gauge the health of the market. These are now compiled by a separate company, FTSE International, in conjunction with the Institute and Faculty of Actuaries. FTSE stands for *Financial Times* – Stock Exchange.

The indices cover the UK and foreign markets, and there are indices for both shares and the *fixed interest** markets. The most widely quoted index is the FTSE 100, or Footsie, which was set up in 1984. The FTSE 100 uses as a base the 100 leading British companies, and the constituents are reviewed every quarter. Although there are more than 3,000 companies listed, these 100 blue chips account for around 75 per cent of the total capitalisation of the UK market, and so are a good barometer of investor sentiment. The Footsie is a real-time index and its value is recalculated every 15 seconds – the other main UK share indices are calculated every minute.

The other most scrutinised index is the FTSE All-Share which covers 98 per cent of the main market by capitalisation – around 865 stocks. The All-Share, is calculated as an arithmetic mean of about 800 shares. These are broken down into different industrial groups and within them are sectors, to enable investors to track the progress of different areas within the index.

So, for example, within the 'Mineral Extraction' group are sectors for 'Extractive Industries', 'Oil, Integrated' and 'Oil Exploration & Production'. The weightings of the constituent companies are calculated according to their market capitalisation, meaning that movements in large companies' shares will have more impact on the index than those of smaller companies. Thus, if shares in a large company rise by 5 per cent in a day, it will have a greater effect on the index than if a small company rises by the same amount. As well as showing price movements, the index shows average *yields**.

Both the FTSE 100 and the All-Share are used extensively for *index tracker funds** – investment funds which aim to follow the ups and downs in the market.

In 1992, a new set of indices was introduced to give greater visibility to medium and smaller company sectors. The new indices are the FTSE Mid 250, the FTSE Actuaries 350, and the FTSE SmallCap Index, and they were developed by a working party of investors, actuaries, and representatives from the London Stock Exchange and the *Financial Times*. The FTSE Mid 250 covers the 250 largest companies outside the FTSE 100; the FTSE Actuaries 350 combines the FTSE 100 and the FTSE Mid 250, which together represent about 90 per cent of the value of the UK equity market; and the FTSE SmallCap Index comprises about 450 smaller companies. In 1995, a further index for even smaller companies was launched. The FTSE Fledgling follows the remaining 2 per cent of main market not included in the FTSE All-Share. An index has also been introduced following AIM*.

Indices are also available to follow the different industrial sectors within the market. One of the latest is a sports index to follow the various football companies coming to the market in recent years.

The chief international index is the FT World Index, available including and excluding the UK. FTSE International compiles around 2,000 indices following foreign markets. These are available following markets in local currency and also in sterling terms.

Fixed interest

A number of stockmarket investments pay fixed-interest returns to investors, the most important type being *gilts**, which are *bonds** issued by the British government. Bonds are also issued by companies and local authorities, and companies can also issue *debentures**, which are loans secured on assets, and unsecured loans.

All these securities have a fixed repayment date, and the interest rate they pay will depend on factors such as interest rates at the time of issue, prospects for interest rates, and the perceived credit risk attached to the bonds. Interest on bonds is usually paid half-yearly.

One advantage of fixed-interest investments is that people who need income know exactly how much they will receive and can budget accordingly. But there is also a risk that the fixed return may not keep pace with the rate of *inflation**.

Bonds and loan stocks can be traded on the *stock exchange**, and although they have a fixed repayment price (the 'par' value), the market price can fluctuate according to supply and demand. Prices are largely driven by interest rate movements, which make the fixed interest payment more or less desirable.

A hybrid form of fixed-interest security is the *convertible**, which can be converted at a set time from a bond into a share.

Fixed-interest investments can also be found outside the stockmarket, for example the annuities and guaranteed income bonds issued by insurance companies, fixed-interest deposit accounts at banks and building societies, and some of the National Savings products issued by the Government.

Fledgling

A newly-listed company. By their nature fledgling companies are generally very small. Around 800 companies on the UK main stockmarket are classed as fledglings, accounting for just 2 per cent of the market's capitalisation. Their performance is monitored by the FTSE Fledgling Index.

Flotation

The process of bringing a company to the stockmarket for the first time. See *New issues**.

Footsie

City slang for the FTSE 100 Index of the UK's 100 leading shares. See *FTSE indices**.

Foreign shares

Diversification is an important principle in investment. As its name suggests, it refers to the necessity of building up a good spread of holdings in your portfolio. This involves balancing *shares** with some *bonds** or cash, balancing smaller companies with *blue chips**, and *cyclical stocks** with *defensive stocks**. And it also requires balancing UK investments with some holdings overseas, so that if the UK hits a prolonged *bear** run, you will have some shares in countries where the stockmarket is rising healthily.

One way to get exposure to foreign markets is through British companies that have substantial operations overseas. So one method of accessing the booming economies of the Far East is to invest in British engineering and building companies that have won infrastructure contracts. However, the UK share price will also be influenced by domestic activities, and so this method may be too indirect.

Another way is to buy overseas shares. Although the US is the giant of all domestic stockmarkets, the London Stock Exchange is the world's largest international stock exchange with more overseas companies listed than any other exchange. Key foreign stockmarkets include Hong Kong, Germany, France, Canada, Australia and Switzerland. In addition, there are other, smaller stockmarkets which become very attractive at certain times – Finland, for example, was highly successful and popular in the mid-1990s – including the new generation of emerging markets in Latin

America, the Far East, and Central and Eastern Europe.

Unfortunately, investing in overseas markets can be beset with difficulty for the private investor. First, there is a currency risk, and any gains you make can be wiped out by exchange rate movements between sterling and the currency of the stockmarket involved (although, of course, currency movements can also enhance your gains if you are lucky). Then there are the difficulties posed by language barriers and by different legal systems governing sharedealing and purchases.

The third pitfall is that stockmarkets differ from each other in more than just the companies listed and the languages spoken. One important distinguishing characteristic of each market is volatility, a quality that makes Far Eastern markets such as Hong Kong and Singapore much more of a rollercoaster ride than the UK stockmarket.

There are added risks when it comes to smaller and *emerging markets**. A market with a relatively small number of stocks and a small trading volume is likely to be volatile because dealing, even in smallish quantities, can have an exaggerated effect. In addition, it can be difficult to find buyers for stocks, so you may find yourself stranded with an unwanted portfolio of shares. Emerging markets are also very vulnerable to shifts in investor confidence. For example, in 1994 the Mexican stockmarket fell sharply, and other Latin American markets also dived as investors lost confidence. More recently, Asia suffered the same domino effect.

All these issues mean that for most investors, investing in overseas stocks is easier and safer if it is done through a *unit trust** or *investment trust**.

Fundamentals

A term used by stockmarket analysts when talking about a stockmarket's economic outlook. The fundamentals of a market include interest rates, its currency, inflationary prospects, borrowing requirements, industrial production levels and consumer spending.

Fundamental analysis

Attempts to predict future price movements by looking at a company's current and likely future earnings, the outlook for the industry it is in, its management and plans for growth. Conversely *technical analysis** looks at share price movements to predict where a share is going next and therefore relies on looking at behaviour within the stockmarket as a whole.

Futures

Futures contracts allow those who regularly buy and supply goods to protect themselves (or hedge) against future changes in prices. Contracts were originally taken out on commodities such as tea but can now be taken out on *shares** and on financial instruments such as stockmarket indices and currencies.

A futures contract specifies a quantity of the commodity, share or index, the price and the delivery date. A tea supplier could agree to buy 10,000 tonnes of Darjeeling for £1,000 in three months' time. If the market price rises to £1,100 he has done well; if it falls to £900, he has lost out, but at least the price uncertainty was removed.

A futures contract commits the user to buy or sell the goods in question when the delivery date arrives, unlike an *option**, which does not impose any obligation to buy or sell. However, most traders open and close the contract before the delivery date.

To buy a future, you put down a fraction of the total value, usually 10 per cent, which is known as the margin. In this way, *gearing** is introduced and any increase or decrease in the value of the contract is magnified. If you put down a margin of 12.5 per cent, you have eight times gearing, so a 10 per cent rise in the contract's value represents a return of 80 per cent on the money put down. However, a substantial fall in price can wipe out your initial margin and more, and this is where the very large risk element comes into futures.

Because futures are deemed unsuitable for the majority of private investors, many private client stockbroking firms will not deal in them.

Gearing

The amount of money a company has borrowed, usually expressed as a percentage of its net assets. Gearing is a term frequently used in connection with investment trusts which, unlike unit trusts, have a lot of freedom to borrow money to invest in order to amplify returns for shareholders. However, gearing can be risky, and if markets move the wrong way it will also magnify losses. Most companies look to keep gearing below 20 per cent, so a company with net assets of £1 million, would borrow no more than £200,000.

Gearing can also refers to any investment where the investor takes a small stake but gains the benefit of, or the liability for the whole investment. *Futures** are highly-geared investments.

Gilts

When the UK government needs to raise money to fund public expenditure, it issues *bonds** known as gilt-edged securities, gilts or British government stock. They are called gilts because, in the past, they were issued as certificates with a gilt edging, although some people argue it is because these bonds are so safe they were considered 'good as gold'.

Gilts are often referred to as part of the *fixed interest** market, but some issues pay index-linked returns. Because they are backed by the Government, they are a very stable investment and the risk of default is extremely low.

Gilts have a par or face value, usually £100. Most are 'dated', which means that the par value is repaid on a fixed date. There are three categories of dated stock: short-dated stock, or shorts, has a life of five years or less; medium-dated stock lasts five to 15 years, and long-dated stock has a life of 15 years or more.

The rate of interest, known as the coupon, is expressed as a percentage of the par value. Interest is usually paid every six months, and is paid gross (without tax deducted), if gilts are bought directly, e.g. to a Post Office, but net of tax if purchased through an intermediary, e.g. a stockbroker.

Gilts are traded on the *Stock Exchange** and can sell at more or less than their par value. The *Financial Times* carries all details of tradable gilt stocks. If you turn to the Companies & Market section and look under International Capital Markets, you will find the prices for the whole gilt market. The first column shows the name of the gilt and the date on which it matures, so Treasury Stock 13% 2000 will pay 13 per cent gross a year and be redeemed in 2000.

The next column, listed 'Int', shows the interest *yield** – the rate of interest relative to its market price. If Treasury Stock 13% 2000 had a par value of £100 and a current price of £110, the interest yield would be 11.8 per cent. The next column is the redemption yield, which represents the total yield in terms of both the interest yield and the capital gain or loss that will be made if the gilt is held to redemption. The next column shows the gilt's current market price. If this is more than the par value it is said to be at a premium, and if below, it is said to be at a discount to par. The final column shows the highest and the lowest price on that gilt during this year.

The biggest influences on a gilt's price are the fluctuation in short-term interest rates and supply and demand. When base rates rise, gilt prices fall. For example, the price of Treasury Stock 13% 2000 will fall if 15 per cent is available elsewhere. Just the expectation that general interest rates are going to rise can push down the price of gilts, so investors have to keep a close eye on the economy. In general, long-dated gilts are more volatile than short-dated gilts.

Gilts can be bought through a *stockbroker**, or from the *National Savings Stock Register** either direct or through a post office.

Growth stock

A share which is expected to see rapid growth in share price over a sustained period of time.

Growth stocks are characteristically smaller companies which are expanding rapidly, often in a dynamic sector of the market such as technology. Because they are using money to expand their business, dividends are generally small.

Hedging

The practice of protecting oneself against downside risk, be it the fall in a share price or the rise in inflation.

Hedging instruments include *futures** and *options**. By arranging a futures contract to take delivery of a share, currency or commodity at a certain price at a certain date in the future, it is possible to hedge against prices rising between now and then. Investors can hedge against falls in investments they already hold. Say you have a portfolio with a large American exposure but are concerned that your profits in sterling will be diminished because the dollar is going to fall in value. You could write a futures contract that will offer delivery of the dollar at today's rate. If the dollar does fall, the value of the futures contract will rise and cover the loss in the portfolio.

A common hedge against *inflation** is to buy property or shares, which should keep pace with inflation over the longer term, or index-linked bonds.

High yielding shares

A term given to shares which offer a higher-than-average level of income. Shares pay out income through a half-yearly *dividend**. It tends to be well-established companies which are higher yielders, because younger ventures are more concerned with ploughing their profits back to grow their business. You can assess a company's yield by dividing its share price by its dividend. If a share's yield is substantially higher than the rest of the market, try to find out why. It could be that the share price has dropped recently, making the dividend proportionately larger.

Historic p/e

The *price/earnings ratio** for a share based on its past earnings. Analysts may be just as, if no more, interested in a company's prospective p/e, based on its forecast earnings for the coming financial year.

Hoare Govett indices

Most of the stockmarket indices followed by investors are compiled by FTSE International. However, a few influential indices are compiled by other companies. Stockbroker Hoare Govett's UK Smaller Companies Extended Index is the key measure of smaller capitalised UK companies along with the FTSE SmallCap Index. Many smaller company funds use the Hoare Govett index as a benchmark, only investing in companies which fall below the capitalisation of its largest constituent.

IMRO

Stands for Investment Management Regulatory Authority. See *Regulation**.

Income tax

Income from investments are currently taxed at two rates: a basic rate of 20 per cent and 40 per cent for higher-rate taxpayers. In many cases, income from investments is paid out 'net', i.e. with the basic rate already deducted so basic-rate taxpayers have no further tax to pay. Higher-rate taxpayers then pay their further 20 per cent liability through their tax return.

Non-taxpayers can reclaim the 20 per cent basic-rate tax paid on investments, or in the case of savings accounts and *gilts** they can register to receive interest without any tax deducted (i.e. gross). The tax on share dividends is accompanied by a 20 per cent tax credit. Currently, this credit can be reclaimed by non-taxpayers but only until April 1999, at which point the tax credit drops to 10 per cent, and can only be reclaimed by investments held in PEPs and ISAs. The reduction in the tax dividend ties in with the phasing out of *Advance Corporation Tax**.

Independent financial adviser

A term which came into being with the 1986 Financial Services Act polarising financial advisers into two camps: those that are tied to one product provider – usually a life assurance company – and can only advise on its products, and **independent** financial advisers (IFAs) who have no such ties and are free, indeed are obliged, to scour the market for the best product for a client's needs.

IFAs can advise on and arrange pensions, PEPs, unit trusts and investment trusts, life assurance-based products and savings vehicles. However, to advise and trade in individual shares they must be qualified as a stockbroker and have the relevant exams from the Securities Institute (the only exception being the shares of investment trust companies which can be bought through the trust's own savings scheme).

Index

Anyone wishing to follow the performance of a particular stockmarket over a day, a month or a period of years should consult a relevant market index which tracks the rises and falls in value. There are a number of share indices covering some or all of the shares in the London stockmarket, and others covering other assets including fixed-interest bonds and commodities. The most widely used are the *FTSE Indices**, with the FTSE All-Share and the FTSE 100 being the most commonly-used gauges of stockmarket trends.

Beyond London, there are indices covering the other stockmarkets of the world, ranging from the very influential *Dow Jones Industrial Average** of 30 large US manufacturing companies, and *Standard & Poor's** Composite Index of all common stocks traded on the New York Stock Exchange to Japan's *Nikkei** indices, the German DAX and France's CAC-40. Apart from these homegrown indices, the *Financial Times* and the London Stock Exchange are responsible for indices covering foreign markets, one of the latest major editions being the FTSE Eurotop 300, following the 300 largest European companies. The FT in conjunction with Standard & Poor's is also responsible for the FT/S&P-A World Index, which aims to give a picture of the movements of markets across the world.

As well as indicating the value of particular shares, sectors and markets, indices underlie and act as a benchmark for many investments. Institutional investors such as pension funds which require steady growth may have indexed portfolios which buy stocks in the same proportions as they are represented in, say, the FTSE 100. *Index-tracking** funds have a similar objective and, because they aim to reduce the investor's vulnerability to falls in specific sectors or companies, they are often held to be a good point of entry to equity investment. In a more esoteric vein, *futures** and *options** contracts can 'buy' or 'sell' an index at a certain level at a certain point in the future, and are often used by investments such as guaranteed stockmarket bonds and guaranteed growth bonds which guarantee certain levels of growth to investors.

Index-linked stocks

To hedge against inflation, some investments provide a return linked to the Retail Price Index – the measure of inflation in the UK.

Chief among these are index-linked *gilts**. These have a *redemption** value (the value that is repaid when the *bond** matures) adjusted for the effect of inflation, so that, for example, a bond priced at £100 would repay £200 if prices doubled over its lifetime. The interest paid by the gilt will also increase according to the rate of inflation.

Index-linked gilts usually pay a lower interest rate than conventional gilts, but are likely to produce a higher capital gain. The choice of whether to buy the index-linked or the conventional variety depends on two main factors: prospects for inflation over the term of the bond (the higher the likely rate, the more attractive the index-linked version), and whether capital gain or income is more important. One solution for a fairly cautious portfolio is to go for a balance and to hold some of each. Because index-linked gilts provide a lower income, they are a useful holding for higher-rate taxpayers.

As well as issuing index-linked gilts, the Government is also responsible for Index-linked Savings Certificates, issued by the Department of National Savings. These five-year tax-free investments pay a fixed rate of interest (2.5 per cent in spring 1998) each year plus a return equivalent to the annual rate of inflation.

Index trackers

An index fund, or index tracker, is a *unit trust** that does exactly what its name suggests: it imitates the performance of a market *index** such as the FTSE All-Share Index in the UK. Most investors buy a UK unit trust because they want to achieve at least the same level of growth as the UK stockmarket; the problem is how to avoid the *shares** that underperform the market. By mirroring the index as a whole, they can avoid problems associated with particular companies or particular market sectors, and are reasonably assured of not performing much worse than the market.

Index funds follow an index in one of three ways. The first method is to replicate the index fully by buying every share in the index in the correct proportions. The second method is partial replication: through computer programs and sampling techniques, managers can match the price movements of the index without buying every share. Other trackers don't buy the underlying shares but *futures** contracts, which track the 'price' of the index, with the value of the contract producing returns similar to that of the index.

Individual Savings Account

Announced by the Government in its July 1997 Budget and finalised in its March 1998 Budget, Individual Savings Accounts are the successor to *Personal Equity Plans (PEPs)** and Tax Exempt Special Savings Accounts (TESSAs) and will be open for business from April 1999, at which point any existing PEPs and TESSAs will be ring-fenced.

The idea is to encourage more people to save. The Government is calling on outlets such as supermarkets and credit unions to offer accounts, as well as more traditional investment providers.

Whereas PEPs were predominantly share-based investments, ISAs will be able to hold cash and life-assurance-based investments such as friendly society bonds. However, there are to be strict rules as to how much you can hold in these investments.

Up to £5,000 a year can be invested in an ISA (in the first year only (1999/2000), investment will be increased to £7,000). Of this, a maximum of £1,000 can go into cash investments (in the first year, the cash limit will be £3,000) and £1,000 can go in life assurance products. Any amount up to the annual limit can go in equity and fixed-interest investments, be they held directly or indirectly through an investment funds such as a unit trust. Unlike

PEPs there is no geographical limitation. The only stipulation is that securities must be listed on a recognised stock exchange. Shares without a stockmarket listing, or which are listed on the Alternative Investment Market will not be admitted. Also, shares acquired through a public offer or received when a building society demutualises cannot be transferred into an ISA (PEPs did accept such shares provided they were transferred within 42 days.)

As with PEPs, all income and gains on investments are tax-free and need not be declared on a tax return. There is no time limit for holding investments in an ISA to qualify for the tax breaks, although product providers are likely to impose their own conditions. As well as PEPs, ISAs are also superseding TESSAs. Any existing TESSAs will be able to run for their full term, at the end of which the capital in the account can be transferred to an ISA, in addition to that year's ISA allowance.

Inflation

Inflation is the tendency for prices to rise. The rate of inflation measures the degree by which they rise. In the UK, the official indicator of inflation is the Retail Price Index (RPI), which is calculated each month by the Office of National Statistics from a representative sample of goods and services around the country. Each month the index calculates how much the cost of these items has risen. Since the index covers the preceding 12 months, the inflation rate quoted is always backward-looking. *Index-linked* investments such as index-linked *gilts* pay returns linked to the RPI. High inflation is a cause for concern for anyone on a fixed income or living on the income from capital, because it quickly erodes the real value of that income and of the capital. For example, if the rate of inflation was 10 per cent for five years, £1,000 would be worth the equivalent of £621 after five years. After ten years, it would be worth the equivalent of just £386. Consequently, keeping pace with or outstripping inflation is seen as a priority for many investors and portfolio managers.

Low inflation has been one of the Government's guiding economic principles during the last decade. The most important brake on inflation is interest rates. By raising bank interest rates, the Bank of England can increase the cost of borrowing and therefore dampen consumer spending, which can in turn contain the cost of goods. High inflation and interest interest rates tend to go hand in hand, which is why often in periods when interest rates have been high (for example in the early 1990s in the UK) the real rate of return once the rate of inflation is taken into account can be much lower.

Inheritance tax

Inheritance tax is payable on certain possessions ('your estate') when you die, including savings and investments. Everyone has an inheritance allowance, before any tax is payable. In 1998/99 this is set at £225,000, which sounds a lot, but even a modest-sized family property (or even a small flat in some parts of London) can tip you over this limit, at which point tax is payable at a flat rate of 40 per cent. Individuals can reduce the tax bill payable by their heirs by making gifts before they die. These are called potentially exempt transfers because, depending when they are made, they may be exempt from inheritance tax. Gifts made more than three years before death are charged at 80 per cent of the full rate (i.e. 32 per cent), those made more than four years before death are charged at 60 per cent of the full rate and the rate reduces for each year so that gifts made more than seven years before death are exempt from inheritance tax.

In addition, you can make gifts of up to £3,000 year, and make as many 'small gifts' as you want, provided they don't exceed £250 per person per year.

Insider dealing

An illegal practice of using privileged information to trade to your advantage in advance of the rest of the market. What constitutes insider dealing is a very grey area. But the London Stock Exchange imposes strict regulations to stop it happening.

For a start, all share price-sensitive information must be relayed initially through the Exchange's Regulatory News Service (*RNS**) so it reaches all brokers at exactly the same time.

Second, company directors and employees are subject to a 'closed period' and cannot deal in shares in their own company in the run-up to company results being announced.

Thirdly, members of the Stock Exchange are policed by very strict rules as to what they can buy and sell for their own purposes, and investment firms must be able to demonstrate *Chinese Walls** between their different departments so there is not an easy exchange of information between say, the stockbroking arm and the corporate financing department.

Finally, the Exchange is on the look out for unusual trades each and every day. Moreover, it is not averse to looking at share-dealings retrospectively, say trades which took place as long as six months or a year ago. If it turns out that, say, a company director offloaded a large chunk of his shares just before an announcement which rocked the share price, he or she could quickly find himself under investigation.

Institutional investors

As opposed to private investors, institutional investors are the managers of life assurance and pension funds, each one having perhaps billions of pounds under management. The behaviour of institutional investors is important to watch, because their decisions can sway the market. If the institutions decide to move out of a part of the market, the sell-off in shares can see prices tumble. A close watch is often kept on the institutionals' holdings in cash. If they go 'overweight' in cash it can be there is a general consensus that equities are looking overvalued and are due for a 'correction'.

Many commentators believe it is the institutional investors that have driven the bull market since 1994/95. As more individuals have to make private provision for retirement, particularly as state provision is whittled down in areas such as Europe, institutional funds, and therefore demand for equity investment, is likely to grow.

Interims

Company results are issued at two points in the year. 'Finals' are given at the end of the company's year-end, whilst 'interims' are given six months prior to detail the state of the company's first half-year of trading. Each announcement may be accompanied by a *dividend** to shareholders. The interim dividend is authorised by the directors, whereas the final – and usually larger – dividend is recommended by the directors but must be authorised by the shareholders at the company's *annual general meeting**. Some companies may choose only to give a final dividend, but many prefer to give an interim as well to maintain interest in the shares throughout the year.

Investment banking

The term given to that area of the bank concerned with corporate activities such as advising on mergers and acquisitions and raising long-term loans and equity capital for companies. In the US there has legally been a delineation between investment banks (or merchant banks as they are better known in the UK) and commercial banks concerned with deposit-taking and retail business, which is enforced under the Glass-Steagal Act. However, the barriers between the two types of institution are starting to crumble, leading to the mega-mergers between many of the big banking names.

Many UK banks have investment banking and retail arms. However, in recent years, some have sold off their investment banking divisions, claiming retail banking to be more profitable.

Investment clubs

The idea of investment clubs originated in the US as a way for private investors to get together and pool their money and ideas in order to manage a portfolio of shares. Now they are popular the world over as a way for investors to dip a toe in the stockmarket, who on their own might not have had the money nor confidence to do so.

A group of investors (no more than 20 in the UK) meets regularly, and each person puts in a small subscription to buy holdings. At meetings, members discuss possible and existing investments, perhaps giving each member the responsibility to research a *share** or a sector.

In the UK, *ProShare**, an organisation set up to encourage wider share ownership, is an enthusiastic advocate of investment clubs, and publishes a manual explaining how to set up and run an investment club. It also runs a 'lonely hearts' investment column in its magazine which helps to put would-be investment club members in touch with clubs that have vacancies. By 1998, there were approximately 2,000 investment clubs in the UK affiliated to ProShare.

The ProShare manual provides a standard set of rules that enable members to meet various legal requirements, but beyond these requirements, it is up to members how they organise their activities. ProShare reports that the clubs are increasingly popular among the recently retired, who have plenty of time to meet and to read up about the markets, but there are also many examples of other groups who have set up a club, ranging from oil rig workers on Brent Bravo to members of Blackburn Golf Club, to regulars of a pub near Macclesfield.

Clubs also vary in the width of their investment parameters, some confining their activities to *FTSE 100** shares, others to companies that meet green and ethical criteria, while one strategy that can be effective is to invest in areas of which the group has special knowledge, for example a club of nurses or doctors might specialise in pharmaceuticals.

The ProShare investment club manual is available from ProShare Investment Clubs at Library Chambers, 13-14 Basinghall Street, London EC2V 5BQ.

Investment trusts

Investment trusts (ITs) are companies set up to buy shares in other companies. Anyone who buys shares in an investment trust is indirectly buying dozens or even hundreds of different shares. For the private investor, buying ITs is likely to be less risky than investing the same amount of money in individual equities, because of the principle of diversification. Investment trusts which invest overseas, either globally or in specific regions, give investors the chance to gain exposure to international stockmarkets that would otherwise be inaccessible. In these respects, investment trusts have a similar function to *unit trusts**.

Some of the longest-standing ITs are generalist trusts which invest globally. A look at the past portfolios of these trusts reveals that enthusiasm for *emerging markets** investment is nothing new, since some trusts have been investing in regions like Asia since the nineteenth century.

Other trusts concentrate on one country such as the UK or Japan, or a region such as North America or the Pacific Basin. Some funds invest in one particular sector such as commodities and energy. More specialist still are trusts investing in the Lloyd's insurance market. One variation on the IT theme, called the *venture capital trust**, even attracts special tax concessions. Some of the more specialised investment trusts, such as those investing in a single emerging market, are aimed at other institutional investors as well as at the public, and prices can be very volatile.

Investment trusts can offer income, capital growth or a mixture of the two. *Split capital investment trusts** offer different classes of share to cater for different investment objectives. Both standard and split capital investment trust shares can be held in a *personal equity plan (PEP)**, so long as more than 50 per cent of the trust is invested in ordinary shares listed on a recognised EU stock exchange or in eligible *corporate bonds**, *preference shares** and *convertibles**. Those that do not reach this threshold are limited to a maximum of £1,500 out of the annual £6,000 general PEP allowance. Some trusts, including some emerging markets ITs, are not eligible for PEPs at all.

Investment trusts can be bought through *stockbrokers** and other financial advisers, or direct from the IT managers themselves. Most trusts accept both lump sums and regular monthly contributions. The minimum lump sum accepted is usually £250-£500, although a few require more, and minimum monthly savings are usually £25-£50 although, again, some require more and a few do not accept monthly contributions.

One advantage of the regular savings route is that investors do not have to grapple so hard with questions of market timing (i.e. when to buy the shares). They also benefit from a principle called *pound/cost averaging** which means that the average cost of the shares over a period of time will be less than their average price (this applies to unit trusts and shares as well as investment trusts).

Although there are similarities between unit trusts and investment trusts, there are also differences. One difference is the way they are priced. The price of unit trusts depends directly on the value of the assets held by the trust, but because ITs are companies, the price is also influenced by supply and demand. As a result, the share price of an IT may be the same, higher or lower than the value of the underlying capital of the trust (the *net asset value** or NAV) divided by the number of shares. If the shares are trading at a price higher than the NAV per share, the trust is said to be at a premium; if they are trading below the NAV per share, it is trading at a discount. A discount can mean that the investor is getting good value, but it can also mean that the share is not in demand, perhaps because the market does not rate its prospects or management. Most trusts trade at a slight discount to NAV. Investment trust share prices and NAVs are listed in the *Financial Times*.

Another difference from unit trusts is that ITs, being companies, can borrow money. This can help a trust to produce high returns, but it also makes the fund more risky. A further difference is that they can invest in unlisted shares (see *Listing**). Again, this can be high-risk, and many trusts do not avail themselves of the opportunity.

ISA - See *Individual Savings Account**

Investment fund

An investment vehicle which pools investors' money and spreads it across many different holdings. Investment funds include *unit trusts**, *investment trusts**, *OEICs**, and pension funds.

Investors' Compensation Scheme

A scheme funded by all firms regulated under the *Financial Services Authority**. The Investors' Compensation Scheme covers investors for up to £48,000 if a regulated firm goes out of business and loses any of their monies in the process. See *Regulation**

Jobbers

Before *Big Bang** in October 1986, members of the *stock exchange** had to be either *stockbrokers** or stockjobbers (or brokers and jobbers). The former bought and sold stocks and *shares** for the public, while the latter worked from stalls on the stock exchange floor and acted as a wholesaler, buying from and selling to the brokers. Jobbers tended to specialise in certain areas, although the bigger firms would operate across a whole range of areas.

Since Big Bang, the distinction between the two types has disappeared, and a firm can both make a market in stocks and deal direct with public. Because of the change, the term jobber is no longer used, and those who make a market in stocks and shares are now given the more self-explanatory title of *market-maker**.

Junk bonds

Bonds* are issued by governments, local authorities and companies to raise money. Different bonds carry different levels of risk. The lowest-risk category are government bonds, such as UK *gilts**, because the likelihood of the government being unable to repay your capital is very low. Corporate bonds are higher-risk because there is a bigger chance of default. The highest-risk corporate bonds are called junk bonds, and they are issued by, for example, small companies or companies in a fairly precarious financial state. The investor who buys junk bonds accepts that there is a very high risk of default and in return receives a very high *yield**.

Junk bonds enjoyed a period of popularity in the US during the 1980s, and were often used as part of the financing for leveraged buyouts.

LIFFE

Pronounced 'life' and stands for London International Financial Futures & Options Exchange – the exchange on which *derivatives** are traded in the UK.

You can set up an *option** or *futures** contract via your stockbroker provided they are a member of LIFFE. The broker will telephone LIFFE, where a trader will write the contract. Whereas the London Stock Exchange now deals on a completely automated basis, LIFFE still has a 'floor' where trading takes place in the day. The LIFFE trading floor is extremely colourful as those present have to wear different coloured jackets to indicate who they are. Traders wear red jackets, administrative staff wear yellow and LIFFE staff, who do not trade, wear blue. Traders signal deals through a mixture of hand signals and shouting.

Once the floor is closed, trading continues via computer on the Automated Pit Trading system (APT), and there are plans to computerise some of LIFFE's daytime trading.

Limit order

If you want to leave an order with your stockbroker to buy or sell a certain stock but you don't want to go above or below a certain price, you can place a limit order, indicating the lowest price you will go to if you are selling, or the highest price at which you will agree to buy.

Limited liability

When a company issues shares it must do so under the condition that they are for limited liability only. That means a shareholder's losses if the company goes out of business will be limited to their share capital and they cannot be called upon by the company's debtors. The concept of limited liability was introduced in the nineteenth century.

Liquidity

Tends to be used to refer to how easily a company's shares can be turned into cash. Large blue-chip companies tend to have a high level of liquidity and buyers and sellers for their shares can be easily found. Smaller companies, such as those listed on the *Alternative Investment Market**, are less liquid.

Liquid assets can also refer to how much of an *investment portfolio** is being kept in cash.

Listing

Securities* traded on the main *London Stock Exchange** are quoted on the Official List of Securities, and are therefore known as listed or quoted companies. To get a full listing, a company must sign a listing agreement, agreeing to a number of conditions, known as listing requirements, detailed in the *Yellow Book**. For example, the company must have assets of a certain size and must agree to make certain information about its finances available to shareholders in its *annual report & accounts**. The requirements for companies joining the Alternative Investment Market are less stringent than those of the main market.

Other international stock exchanges have their own requirements for listed companies.

Loan stock

Companies' debt or borrowings can take several forms, including bank loans and overdrafts, *debentures**, and loan stocks (also known as *corporate bonds**). Whereas debentures are secured on the assets of the company, loan stock is not secured on anything so it is more risky.

Loan stocks have a fixed date of repayment, and in the meantime most pay a fixed rate of interest. Unsecured loan stocks usually pay a higher rate of interest than both government bonds and debentures because the risk of default is higher. And generally, the higher the perceived risk attached to a company's bonds, the higher the interest rate it will have to pay in order to make the issue attractive to investors.

If the company runs into financial difficulties, unsecured loan stock comes further down the pecking order for repayment than debentures, but above *ordinary shares** and *preference shares**.

Convertible* loan stock can be converted at a set date or within a set period from loan stock into ordinary shares in the company.

Local authority stock

In the UK, local authorities can fund their spending by issuing *bonds**. Some local authority stock, called negotiable yearling bonds, can be traded on the stockmarket. The bonds are usually issued by local authorities once a week and last for a year, or occasionally two years. Interest is fixed for the life of the bond and is paid twice-yearly net of basic-rate tax. Higher-rate taxpayers must pay further tax, while non-taxpayers can reclaim the tax paid.

It is possible to make capital gains or losses on the bonds as well, but because of their short life, they normally trade very close to their face value. The current prices, interest and *redemption* yield** on negotiable stock is given in the *Financial Times* alongside UK *gilts**.

In addition to yearling bonds, local authorities issue fixed-term loans called local authority bonds. These are not tradable on the stockmarket and have an investment term of between one and ten years. Interest is fixed and depends on the term and size of the bond. It is usually paid twice-yearly, again with basic-rate tax deducted. The minimum investment is usually £1,000 but may be lower, at £250 or £500. Local authority bonds can be bought through newspaper coupons or from the local authority treasurer's department.

Both types are useful for investors who need a fixed income, but local authority bonds may be unsuitable for people who may need access to their money within the term of the loan.

Local authority stock cannot be held in *PEPs** or *ISAs**.

London Stock Exchange

The London Stock Exchange has been the platform for dealing in securities in the UK for almost 200 years. In the late 1760s a group of stockbrokers formed a subscription club at Jonathan's Coffee House, later opening their own premises, New Jonathan's, in Threadneedle Street. In 1773, the name was changed to The Stock Exchange, and has been based on its current site of Old Broad Street since 1801.

The London Stock Exchange provides two markets for

companies wishing to raise capital and for investors wishing to trade in the shares of those companies: the main market and the *Alternative Investment Market** for smaller, young and growing companies.

To deal in stocks and shares, *stockbrokers** must be members of the London Stock Exchange. To do so, they must demonstrate suitable qualifications, competency and financial stability. However, there is no compunction to be based in London, and the LSE has more than 270 members spread across the UK, including Northern Ireland and Scotland.

Over the last decade, the way the London Stock Exchange operates has undergone something of a revolution. Until 1986, trading actually took place on the floor of the Stock Exchange in the City, and there was a two-tier trading system of *jobbers** and *stockbrokers**.

Since *Big Bang** in 1986, share-trading has been screen-based using a system known as *SEAQ** (Stock Exchange Automated Quotations system) which allows members of the London Stock Exchange to trade directly with one another.

All companies trading on the Stock Exchange must appear on the Official List of Shares. Entry to the List entails fulfilling certain *listing** requirements concerning capitalisation and the company's accountability.

Long position

A *market-maker** or investor who is optimistic about a share (or other holdings such as a currency) might build up a long position in that holding. This means building up a large holding of that share, in the expectation of being able to sell it on at a good profit.

The opposite of going long is going short, a strategy adopted by someone who believes the price of a share will go down. The market-maker or speculator who 'sells short' sells stock he or she does not own, in the expectation of being able to pick it up cheaper later on.

Both strategies are speculative and can be highly risky. Anyone with a long position runs the risk of being landed with large quantities of stock worth less than the price paid for them, while a short position involves the risk of being contracted to sell stock for a price lower than the market price. In either case, losses (and gains if things turn out right) can be substantial.

Managed fund

An investment fund which invests across a well-diversified range of assets. Life companies often refer to their managed fund, by which they mean their flagship unit-linked life assurance or pension fund which invests in their other funds. Some companies offer a number of managed funds to meet different investors' appetite for risks, classifying them as, for example, cautious, aggressive and balanced.

Management buy-out

The acquisition of a company by some of its own managers. MBOs often arise where a large company wants to divest itself of part of its business.

Margin

The difference between the prices at which a *market-maker** will buy and sell a particular stock or share. The margin, or jobber's turn, is the way a market-maker makes his income. However the introduction of *SETS**, whereby buy and sell orders are matched and no intermediary is required, is expected to force margins to narrow, if not disappear completely.

Also refers to the 10 per cent payment a buyer puts down to take possession of an *option** contract. In share-dealing, an investor might deposit a margin with a stockbroker to cover any losses he expects to make.

Market influences

The price of *stocks** and *shares** is governed by supply and demand, and these themselves are influenced by many factors, some of them logical and others not so logical, some of them related to the company itself and others related to events outside the company.

One obvious influence on a company's share price is the company's own activities and prospects, for example its annual profits or expected annual profits, a takeover bid, or the appointment of a new chief executive who is much admired in the City.

Others are more general, and include economic data. Good employment figures, for example, may benefit the share price because they may herald a rise in consumer confidence and spending, while a rise in interest rates may be harmful because it will raise the cost of borrowing and damage consumer confidence. Politics also comes into play, and an imminent general election and uncertainty about a future government can lead to stockmarket jitters and sometimes turbulence. Global politics and economics are all important, with events in the US and anything that threatens oil supplies having a particular bearing.

Finally, the market influences itself. On a small scale, dealers can cause a share price to drop by profit-taking (selling stocks to realise a gain), and on a medium scale, the City rumour mill, spreading whispers about takeovers or profit warnings, can send a share price soaring upwards or downwards, often leading to accusations of insider dealing. On a far bigger scale, the herd instinct of the City means that *bear** markets and *bull** markets can be self-perpetuating, and lead to a stampede.

Market-makers

Until 1986, there were two tiers of trading in the *London Stock Exchange**. The first, the *jobbers**, would buy and sell shares on their own behalf and could not deal directly with the public. Instead they dealt with the second group, *stockbrokers**.

In 1986, at *Big Bang**, the distinction between the groups was broken down, and a firm could act in either capacity. The successor to the jobber is the market-maker, who acts as a wholesaler of *shares** and sets the buying and selling prices for securities. They have a duty to make a continuous market in the shares in which they deal, thus ensuring that markets remain liquid. Like jobbers, they make their money on the turn – that is, by selling shares for slightly more than they would be prepared to buy them for.

However, market-making could be a dying trade. Under the *SETS** system of share-trading introduced in 1997 and used initially to trade in *FTSE 100** stocks, orders to buy and sell shares are matched automatically, obviating the need for an intermediary. However, many stockbrokers may continue to prefer to use the old market-making system at least for some trades, because they believe they can get keener prices. Market-makers do not just function in the sphere of stocks and shares. Some, mainly banks, make a market in currencies, and a few firms make a market in second-hand endowment policies. Whichever area market-makers specialise in, they are essential to the efficient functioning of the market.

Market sectors

Take a look at the London *share** prices in a newspaper like the *Financial Times*, and you will see that the shares are divided into a number of sectors, such as building & construction, property, retailers (food), retailers (general), extractive industries and so on. You will also find a list of the five best-performing sectors of the previous day and the five worst-performing.

These different sectors do not all behave in the same way, with some, like oil exploration and production, likely to be more volatile than others such as food retailers. Different sectors also respond in different ways to the economic and political climate; for example, when Labour took power, some commentators forecast that the construction sector would benefit, while the utilities and financial sectors might suffer.

Managers of funds like *unit trusts** adopt different approaches to choosing their holdings, and one method, known as the top-down approach, takes the economic climate as its starting point and works down from there. A top-down manager of a UK fund would judge which sectors are likely to benefit from existing and forthcoming economic conditions in the UK, and then look for companies within those sectors.

Merchant banks

These started life as the financial arms of the 18th century merchant trading houses and were concerned with raising capital for trading overseas. However, merchant banking is now synonymous with the US term, investment banking, and is primarily concerned with helping companies raise long-term loans, acquire other companies or float on the stockmarket.

Apart from corporate financing, many merchant banks have found profitable business in fund management and private banking.

A number of the big names in merchant banking in the UK such as Kleinwort Benson, Morgan Grenfell, and Barings are now owned by larger, foreign financial institutions.

Mergers and acquisitions

A takeover bid, or even a rumoured takeover bid, can work wonders for a *share** price, since if a company wants to take over another company it normally has to acquire at least 50 per cent of the shares. Once it has acquired 30 per cent of the shares, it has to make a formal offer to the remaining shareholders, usually at a level above the market price in order to make the offer attractive. Occasionally, the shareholders will be offered shares in the predator company rather than cash.

Some areas of the market have seen heavy merger and acquisition activity in recent years. Many banks and financial institutions have made alliances to increase economies of scale, and Europe is expected to see a lot of activity as companies seek to rationalise and become more profitable.

The importance of M&A for the private shareholder is the effect on the share price. We have already noted the beneficial effect of a bid, but there may also be problems: the expense involved may damage the predator's share price, or if the takeover runs into trouble with the Monopolies and Mergers Commission or if the people at the top of each company cannot see eye to eye, any gains in the share price may be wiped out. It is therefore useful for investors to follow events closely in any takeover situation.

Money markets

The wholesale platforms on which banks and other institutions lend money to one another. Private investors can access them through money market unit trusts, where the fund manager will deposit money on the markets to get the best rate of interest, and through money market accounts, which allow money to be deposited and earn interest for short-term periods of one night to three months.

Moody's - see *Credit rating**

Mutual funds

American term for *collective funds**

MSCI World Index

The internationally-used index for following global stockmarkets, and the benchmark used by many international investment funds. The index is compiled by Morgan Stanley (MSCI stands for Morgan Stanley Capital International). It covers all stockmarkets and is weighted so that the markets with the largest stockmarket capitalisation have the largest influence. Because of this it is heavily weighted towards the US and Japan and is therefore not necessarily a good benchmark for UK-based investors who should have their portfolio weighted towards British stocks.

Nap

A piece of horse racing terminology which has passed into investment terminology to mean a promising share tip. *Tip sheets** and the City columns of the financial pages often carry naps, but investors would be well advised to do some sound research into a company before they buy, as there is no recourse to the nap-giver if the tip proves a dud.

NASDAQ

NASDAQ stands for the National Association of Securities Dealers Automated Quotation System, a US computerised trading system established in 1971 and which is now the second-largest stockmarket in the US (the New York Stock Exchange is the largest).

The securities traded are all over-the-counter (OTC) shares, which are bought and sold outside a recognised stockmarket. NSADAQ has terminals throughout Europe and Canada for dealing in US shares.

In addition to its size, NASDAQ's historical importance lies in the fact that it was the first trading system without a market floor, and thus led the way for the elimination of other physical marketplaces, for example the London Stock Exchange floor, in favour of computerised dealing.

National Savings Stock Register

Provides a means of buying British government *gilts** without going through a stockbroker. Members of the public can buy stocks on the NSSR through post offices or directly from National Savings by completing an application form. The maximum that can be purchased in one day is £25,000, although there is no overall limit on holdings.

A drawback of buying direct is that the order can take longer to effect than if you buy through a broker and the price of the stock could move in the meantime. Also, there is no-one working on your behalf to ensure that you get the best price. However, some investors prefer going direct because there is no broker's *commission** to pay.

Net asset value (NAV)

There are two contexts in which you are most likely to encounter the phrase net asset value. The first is if you look at the balance sheet in a company's *annual report and accounts**; the second is if you are thinking of buying shares in an *investment trust**.

The net asset value is an accounting figure that shows the total assets of an organisation less its liabilities and current charges (including *debentures**, *loan stock** and *preference shares**). It basically shows the shareholders' total interest in the company. The net asset value per share divides the NAV by the number of *ordinary shares**. Generally, the NAV per share of a manufacturing company or property company is higher than that of a business that depends on people.

The net asset value is an important factor when choosing an *investment trust**, which is a company that exists solely to invest in other companies. The NAV of an investment trust is the total value of all its assets (i.e. the stocks it owns) after deducting the value of its *preference shares**. The NAV total return measures the performance of an investment trust over a given period and shows the changing value of a trust's assets (assuming net *dividends** were reinvested in the trust).

So, if a trust manager started with £100 and the NAV total return after a year was £120, the manager would have increased the value of the assets by 20 per cent (with income reinvested). Note that investment trust share prices do not directly mirror the NAV total return. If the share price of an investment trust is higher than the net asset value per share, it is said to be at a premium. If it is lower, the shares are said to be at a discount. In spring 1998, investment trust shares were trading at an average discount of 9 per cent to NAV.

New issues

A flotation is the important stage in a company's evolution when it 'goes public' and invites investors to subscribe for its shares. There are several ways for a company to go public, and which it takes depends largely on its size.

Most large companies go public through an 'offer for sale', the route taken by most *privatisation** issues. The shares are offered to the general public through an intermediary such as a *merchant bank**. The company must issue a prospectus, providing information such as a five-year profit and loss statement and a detailed balance sheet.

On an offer for sale, the intermediary handling the sale sets a fixed price for the shares shortly before the flotation. An alternative method is to float the company through a 'tender offer'.

Investors are told the minimum they must bid, and they make their own pitch. Usually, press comment in advance of the flotation will give some idea of suitable bids although, of course, there may be surprises. Both types of listing can end up being very expensive, as a result of fees to merchant banks and lawyers, and smaller companies are permitted to float their shares via a 'placing'. This means that the shares are sold to a selection of, usually institutional, investors through the company's broker.

The benefits of new issues to private investors are that they do not have to pay commission to a *stockbroker** when they buy shares, and the shares are not subject to *stamp duty**. In addition, new issues have often offered good opportunities for profit, since companies often price the issue relatively cheaply in order to attract enough buyers. If this occurs, *stags** can quickly reap good returns by selling the shares immediately at a higher price. But never assume that this will apply to all new issues, since there are also examples of new issue shares having a much lower price a few months after the flotation.

Nikkei 225

The chief index for the Tokyo Stock Exchange and gets its name because it is compiled by the Nikon Keizai Shimbun newspaper group. The 225 securities covered by the index account for around half of the market's total value. You can track the Nikkei 255's movements in the *Financial Times*. The index hit its peak in late 1991 when it almost hit 27,000, but subsequently slid over the next year to fall below 16,000 points in mid-1992. Since then, it has struggled in a trading range of around 21,000, falling again to close to 15,000 during the Asian currency crisis of late 1997.

Nominated adviser

Companies on AIM* enjoy less rigorous regulation than companies on the main market, nevertheless the London Stock Exchange has taken pains to ensure that AIM is maintained as a highly-reputable market. Consequently, if a company wants to get on to the Alternative Investment Market it must do so with the assistance of a nominated adviser, or 'nomad'. The nomad is the duty of the nomad to ensure that the company adheres to the AIM rules. It must ensure that the company's prospectus contains sufficient information for prospective investors to make an informed decision whether to buy and, once the company is trading on AIM, that the company is efficient in divulging information to investors which could affect the share price.

It is in the nomad's interests to ensure that the companies it brings to AIM are appropriate for the market and worthy of investors' attention. If it takes on companies which prove to have a poor level of compliance or are poorly managed, its own reputation will be affected and it may even be removed from the Stock Exchange's register of approved nomads.

AIM companies must maintain a nomad at all times. If a nomad resigns from advising a company, the company has a month to find another nomad or lose its AIM membership.

Nominee account

In June 1995, a new regime for paying for shares, called five-day *rolling settlement**, came into force. Its predecessor was ten-day settlement, which represented a radical change from the system of 'account periods' which was abolished in July 1994.

Five-day rolling settlement means that payment for shares

bought has to be made in five days, and this can be difficult for investors to achieve because of postage times and bank clearing procedures. *Stockbroking** companies are increasingly offering (and some are requiring) the use of nominee accounts to get round the problem. A nominee account is set up by an institution such as a stockbroker, to hold shares and cash for the shareholder. The assets held within the account are legally owned by the company that sets up the account, but the client is the beneficial owner of the assets and of all *dividends** and proceeds that are paid into it.

Nominees can take two forms. A designated nominee means that each investor has their own nominee account, identified by an individual code number, which will be listed on a company's share register when shares are bought. A pooled account will conflate all of a broker's clients' holdings in a particular stock, so the listing on a share register will relate to all of these.

ProShare* has issued a code of practice for nominees. It also has a free factsheet on nominees, which investors can obtain by sending an SAE to ProShare Investor Update (no 2), Library Chambers, 13-14 Basinghall Street, London EC2V 5BQ. The factsheet includes a list of questions that clients should ask before setting up a nominee account, concerning aspects such as security, charges, and access to information.

An alternative to a nominee account for frequent share traders is sponsored membership of *CREST**. This allows shares to be held electronically in the investor's own name. Sponsored membership is only available through stockbrokers with CREST access, and there may be a small annual charge of, typically, £20.

Non-voting shares

One of the rights given to owners of *ordinary shares** is to vote at the company's *annual general meeting**. But a few ordinary shares are non-voting and do not carry that right. Such shares are sometimes called 'A' ordinary shares, and may be slightly cheaper than the voting shares. In addition, you may also come across restricted voting shares, which have a smaller pro rata number of votes. The issue of non-voting and restricted voting shares is discouraged by the *London Stock Exchange**, and they are rare, but you may find them in small companies, for example where a family wants to keep tight control over the family business and keeps the voting shares for its own members.

*Preference shares** do not usually carry voting rights, unless they are in default.

NYSE

Stands for New York Stock Exchange – see *Wall Street**.

OEICs

Until recently, British investors looking for a *investment fund** had a clear-cut choice between unit trusts and investment trusts. Now there is a third option, the open-ended investment company, or OEIC (pronounced 'oik').

OEICs have come about largely because UK investment companies wanted a structure of investment fund familiar to Europeans, which they could market on the Continent. A handful of unit trust providers have converted their unit trusts to an OEIC structure for just this purpose.

An OEIC can be an individual fund or an umbrella vehicle for holding sub-funds. If the OEIC has an umbrella structure, each sub-fund can be marketed to investors individually. Most OEICs are expected to take the umbrella structure, offering a wide range of funds investing in different assets and markets to meet the differing needs of investors. The funds in an OEIC combine elements of both unit trusts and investment trusts. Like investment trusts, they issue shares and so have a corporate structure and can be listed on the Stock Exchange. Also, as with investment trusts, each OEIC fund can offer different classes of share, bestowing on the holder differing rights to capital and/or income from the fund. Shares can also be denominated in different currencies so funds can be sold to foreign investors.

But, like unit trusts, OEIC funds are 'open-ended' so they can alter the number of shares in issue to match demand. Also, the share price is linked directly to the fund's net asset value and moves in tandem with the performance of those assets, rather than being influenced by demand for the fund's shares.

The Association of Unit Trusts and Investment Funds (AUTIF) has hailed OEICs as "a welcome combination of simplicity and flexibility". The simplicity lies in their charging structure. Only one price is quoted rather than the dual pricing (a bid and an offer price) that unit trusts are subject to. Whereas the dual charging structure for unit trusts includes the investment manager's charges and adviser's commission, OEICs show these costs separately so you can see more easily what you are paying for the investment. The manager can vary charges for different subfunds and even for different classes of share.

The investment industry has also lauded the umbrella structure which allows investors to pick and choose their investments very precisely and, says AUTIF, allow funds to organise themselves with "maximum efficiency". The structure also means investors can switch between sub-funds within the same OEIC easily and cheaply, a boon to active investors.

OFEX

A trading facility for those companies that are unable/do not want to be admitted to the *London Stock Exchange** markets. A market in the constituent shares is principally made by just one *market-maker**, JP Jenkins Ltd. Stockbrokers have to approach JP Jenkins if they want to deal in OFEX companies.

OFEX, which was founded in the early 1990s, has really continued where the old Rule 4.2 market left off (see *Rule 4.2 companies**) providing a way of buying and selling illiquid stocks.

Many former Rule 4.2 companies moved to OFEX.

To be included on OFEX, a company must present its report & accounts and other documentation to the OFEX panel. However, there is very little investor protection and the OFEX market must be regarded as extremely high risk. OFEX also warns that since the market is not very *liquid**, it may not be possible to buy and sell at the optimum time. Indeed, many trades are done on a matched bargain basis, with investors making a request to buy or sell and leaving the order until a suitable trade comes along.

Prices for around 120 OFEX companies can be found each day in the *Financial Times*, which lists the mid-market price at the end of the previous day's trading, and the highest and lowest price the stock has reached over the last year.

Offer price

The price at which a *market-maker** is willing to sell a security; the market-maker will always maintain a margin between the offer price and the price at which it is willing to buy the stock (the *bid** price).

Offer document

Sent out to shareholders in the event of a takeover bid. The offer document sets out the terms of the takeover, notably what exchange they will be offered for their shares in the old company, and the arguments for accepting the bid.

Open-ended funds

*Investment funds** such as *unit trusts** and OEICs* which can increase or decrease the number of units or shares in the fund to match investor demand.

Having an open-ended structure is sometimes perceived to be a disadvantage since, if a lot of investors want to sell out of the fund at the same time, the manager will need to sell off investments to give them back their cash, and many not get the best price for those investments. Also, if a lot of investors buy into the fund, it can become unmanageably large. Consequently, many people believe *closed-end** *funds* offer more control.

Options

An option gives you the right to buy or sell a certain *share**, commodity, currency, or *index** such as the *FTSE 100** at a certain price on or by a certain date. Most people's first encounter of options comes from their company in the form of employee share option schemes (see *Employee Share Ownership**) which give them the opportunity to buy shares in the company three to seven years hence at a price fixed when the contract is agreed. Of course, such options are only worth exercising if the *exercise price** is lower than the prevailing market price.

Options are also used in investing. They are generally employed to reduce, or 'hedge', risk in order to limit losses, but they can also be used as an instrument for speculation. Speculative use of options is unlikely to be suitable for the private investor, and many private client *stockbrokers** and investment managers will not deal in them in this way.

*Traded options** are bought and sold on exchanges such as the

London International Financial Futures and Options Exchange (*LIFFE**). The price for a traded option is governed by the demand for that particular option, the value of the underlying security compared with the exercise price, and how much time is left before the option has to be exercised.

Order Book

Under the computerised trading system created under *SETS** stockbrokers can place orders to buy and sell shares. These are maintained on an electronic Order Book which matches buy and sell orders. The Order Book accepts two types of deal. 'At best' orders are to buy and sell shares at the best price available on the book at that time. 'Limit' orders allow investors to set the price at which they are willing to buy and sell but they then may have to wait until a deal at a suitable price comes along.

Ordinary shares

When people talk about shares, they are usually referring to ordinary shares, as opposed to other classes such as *preference shares** or *deferred shares**. Ordinary shares are by far the most common type.

An ordinary shareholder acquires several rights and entitlements when buying a share. They include the right to vote at the *annual general meeting** (except in the case of *non-voting** ordinary shares), and the entitlement to receive a *dividend** payout from the company's profits, if the profits allow. Some ordinary shares also carry shareholder perks – for example, British Airways offers discounts on air fares, P&O offers discounts on cross Channel and other ferries, and Whitbread gives vouchers for use in restaurants and off-licences.

Ordinary shareholders come behind preference shareholders and the owners of *bonds** and *debentures** in the pecking order for repayment if the company goes into liquidation.

Over-the-Counter (OTC)

Name given to any securities market which does not operate through a formal exchange, derived from the practice in the last century in the US of buying *shares** over the counter at banks. OTC markets tend to trade in small, young companies. The largest OTC market is the US's *NASDAQ** market, which is now a highly-respected trading platform and home to the shares of many well-known shares including Microsoft.

Overseas stockmarkets - see *Foreign shares**

Paper

Colloquial name for any security that can be traded, deriving from the fact that ownership is usually registered using a paper certificate (although such a term is becoming a misnomer with the growth in electronic registration and dealing). In the *money markets** paper refers to short-term loan instruments (usually those with less than 90 days' duration), being the most liquid form of borrowing money outside of cash itself.

In a different vein, investors may talk about a paper profit or paper loss when working out the value of their investments. However, they have to sell for the gain or loss to be realised. Reference to a 'paper gain' is used especially where selling will actually result in a loss because of the cost of selling the shares.

Partly-paid shares

Most new *share** issues require investors to pay the whole of the share price at the time of purchase, but a few issues spread the payments so that investors pay in two or three instalments. The best known example was the British Telecom *privatisation**, in which investors paid the first instalment in November 1984, the second in June 1985 and the third in November 1986, with a total of 150p. Investors knew what the two later instalments would be at the time of the issue, but this is not always the case.

A rise in the price of a partly-paid share can introduce 'gearing*', which can produce exaggerated price movements. Take the example of a partly-paid share with instalments of 40p, 30p and 30p, making the full price 100p. The market might believe that the fully-paid issue would be worth 140p, a rise of 40p, and if it does this between the first and second instalments, the price of the share might rise to 80p (the original 40p, plus the 40p extra). The effect is that the partly-paid share shows a gain of 100 per cent, and this is gearing. It can also occur in reverse, producing an exaggerated fall if the share price falls.

The gearing effect disappears once the share becomes fully paid.

Penny shares

Penny share* is the colloquial name given to a share with a very low market price. Generally, penny shares are worth under 10p, although the term is sometimes stretched to 60p.

Penny shares attract investors for a number of reasons. First, because prices are so low, private investors can quickly build up a significant holding in a company. There is no particular advantage to this, but some investors find it satisfying. Second, a rise of just a few pence in the share price can, in percentage terms, have a considerable impact on the share's value and bring good returns.

Another reason is that some investors feel they are getting a bargain. This can be a mistake, for just because the share is cheap, it does not necessarily follow that it is good value. A few penny shares bring large returns when the company turns out to be undervalued, or when it is taken over by a new management team or by another company. But many others have a low share price because they are struggling and will continue to struggle, showing little growth or even folding completely.

Investing in penny shares is therefore a very high-risk way of investing in the stockmarket. If you want to undertake it, detailed information on the company is essential, and you should be prepared to lose your capital if you pick the wrong companies.

Personal equity plans (PEPs)

A personal equity plan (PEP) is a vehicle for buying shares, *unit trusts**, *investment trusts**, *OEICs** and *corporate bonds** which allows investors to receive all income and capital growth tax-free.

PEPs were introduced by the Conservative Government in 1987 as part of its drive to widen share investment, and although they were initially slow to achieve popularity. They now represent a multi-billion pound industry. However, no new PEPs will be available after 5 April 1999, at which point the Labour Government will introduce its successor scheme, the *Individual Savings Account** (ISA).

Until that date, anyone aged 18 or over has a PEP allowance of £9,000, and this is divided into two parts: a £6,000 general allowance which can go into eligible shares, unit trusts and investment trusts, and a £3,000 'single company' allowance. The latter must be invested in one *share**, and was launched partly as a way of boosting employee share-ownership schemes.

All PEPs are administered by a PEP manager, who must be authorised to do so by the Inland Revenue. The PEP manager takes care of administrative tasks such as collecting *dividends** and, because PEPs are tax-free, you do not have to disclose any details of them on your tax return. This makes them a very simple investment in terms of the paperwork and administration connected with them. A wide range of financial institutions manage PEP schemes, and they include banks, fund managers, life assurance companies, and *stockbrokers**. Some offer 'self-select' schemes where the investor chooses the PEP holdings, and others offer a 'managed' or 'discretionary' service, where the manager takes all the investment decisions, working within guidelines such as income, aggressive growth or cautious growth.

Not all shares, unit trusts, and investment trusts are eligible for a PEP. Shares have to be *ordinary shares** or *preference shares** listed on a recognised UK or other EU *stock exchange**. In order to qualify for the full £6,000 general allowance, unit trusts and investment trusts must be at least 50 per cent invested in EU (including the UK) shares, or in corporate and Eurosterling bonds, convertibles and preference shares. Unit trusts and investment trusts which invest more than 50 per cent in shares listed on stockmarkets outside the EU are restricted to no more than £1,500 per year of the £6,000 allowance. And some funds, for example money market funds, *gilt** funds and a few emerging markets funds, are completely ineligible.

Not all the PEPs on the market allow the complete range of eligible holdings. For example, most unit trust and investment trust managers confine their PEPs to their own trusts (there are exceptions), and many share PEPs restrict the choice to the *FTSE 100**, or to UK shares only. So in the event that you want to use a PEP to hold direct equities in continental Europe, you may have to shop around to find a PEP manager which offers this facility.

PEPs are generally subject to three types of charges. There is an initial charge when the plan is set up, an annual management charge, and a dealing charge when, for example, shares are bought and sold. The level of charges varies according to the manager and the nature of investments held in the PEP. Initial charges range between 0 and 6 per cent, annual charges between 0 and 2 per cent, and dealing charges between 0 and 2 per cent.

ISAs are expected to offer much the same features of PEPs, the main differences being the investment limits will be lower, there is no geographical investment restrictions and the new scheme can be used to hold cash deposits. Furthermore, the changes to the tax - credit means it will less advantageous to hold equity investments than was the case with PEPs. Any PEPs in existence after April 1999 can continue to run but no new investment can be made in them. Like ISAs, they will receive a nominal tax credit of 10 per cent until April 2004.

Perks - see *Shareholder Perks**

PIA

The Personal Investment Authority – the organisation responsible for policing financial advisers and the selling and marketing of packaged investments such as pensions, unit trusts and life-assurance based investments such as endowment policies. The functions of the PIA are to be taken over in due course by the newly-formed *Financial Services Authority**.

PIBS

Permanent interest bearing shares (PIBS) are a means for building societies to raise capital. They are a lump sum investment and pay a fixed rate of interest, in most cases twice-yearly.

PIBS are traded on the stockmarket, and their market value depends largely on how the rate of interest paid compares with rates available elsewhere. For example, the first PIBS issued in

1991 paid rates of 13 per cent and more and, when base rates subsequently fell, the market value of these PIBS rose above their face value. Because the capital value can change, the *yield** on PIBS is not necessarily the same as the interest rate paid.

PIBS have no *redemption** date, so to release capital invested in them the investor has to sell them. They are bought and sold through *stockbrokers**.

Interest from PIBS is paid net of 20 per cent income tax. Non-taxpayers can reclaim the tax paid, while 40 per cent taxpayers are liable for a further 20 per cent tax.

The minimum investment in PIBS varies. Some societies issued them with a minimum of £50,000, aiming them primarily at institutional investors, while others have a minimum of £1,000 or £5,000.

One point to watch with PIBS is that, if a building society runs into difficulties and stops or misses interest payments, investors do not qualify for a compensation scheme. However, the chances of a society missing payments are relatively slim.

An added attraction of PIBS these days is the fact that if the society undergoes *demutualisation**, investors, as members of the society, may receive a windfall payment of cash and/or shares. Once a society demutualises, PIBs convert into subordinated debt of the new public limited company.

Placing

The restricted sale of shares on behalf of a company to selected investors, usually *institutional investors**. Placings can provide the means for companies to come to the market for the first time, and after the placing, the shares can be traded in the usual way. Private investors are generally not invited to take part in a placing; their usual avenue to buying new issues is through a *public issue** or *privatisation**.

Portfolio management

Portfolio managers offer several types of service, including *discretionary**, *advisory** and *execution-only** services. Discretionary managers offer more or less bespoke versions of their service, depending on how much money the investor gives them to manage, and they will set up a portfolio based on the investor's requirements such as a low or high risk, and income or growth.

One of the fundamental principles governing the management of any portfolio is the need to attain balance. This can be done in different ways, depending on the desired risk level and objectives, and it means spreading assets across a number of investments so that if one performs badly, others will remain steady or grow. Thus a portfolio may be spread across cash, *bonds** and equities, and the equity component may be spread across different geographical regions and sectors.

The need for balance and *diversification** also explains why portfolio managers often advise investors to buy *unit trusts** and *investment trusts** rather than equities themselves. A well-diversified portfolio needs to comprise about ten or 12 stocks, and the costs of dealing mean that it is not practicable to do this if your portfolio is worth, say, £10,000. Because unit trusts and investment trusts usually hold dozens of different shares, the trust itself offers diversification and balance. Owning two or more trusts with different investment parameters gives investors an excellent spread of holdings and a good balance.

If you are using a professional portfolio manager, who might be an *independent financial adviser**, *stockbroker**, bank, accountant or solicitor who offers investment management, there are several points to watch out for. The first is to make sure that they are authorised by a regulatory body (see **Regulation***) to offer investment advice and to handle your money. You should shop around and talk to several managers, rather than parking all your money with the first one you meet, and you should choose one with whom you feel you could build up a good basis of trust and understanding. You should also make sure you meet the person who will actually manage your portfolio, and not just the marketing manager or one of the directors.

When you do eventually choose a manager, you should expect a grilling. If the manager does not find out all about your assets, financial commitments, goals, family circumstances, aspirations and so on, he or she may not be able to make the right decisions about where to put your money. If you say you want medium risk, for example, make sure you and the manager have the same idea about what medium risk is.

Once you have taken on the manager, you should check up that they are not *'churning*'* your money (i.e. trading too frequently in order to generate commission on the deals), and you should occasionally look at the performance of other investments to see how they compare with the returns on your portfolio.

Pound/cost averaging

A phenomenon enjoyed by investors into *regular savings schemes**, allowing them to benefit from market volatility. If the price of a *share** or investment fund is fluctuating on a regular basis, investors who are drip-feeding a fixed amount of money into the investment over a particular period will buy more shares when the price is low and less when prices are high. Provided, the price ends the chosen period higher than when it had started, the price paid per share or unit will be less than the average price over that time.

For instance, say you invested £30 a month for three months into a share which began with a price of £2, dropped in the second month to £1 then rose in the final month to £2.50. In the first month, your £30 investment buys 15 shares; in month two it buys 30 shares and in the third month you get 12 shares. In total you have 57 shares for an investment of £90 which works out at £1.58 a share. However, the average price of the share over the three months is higher, at £1.83.

Pound/cost averaging works best when prices are very choppy, and primarily where a period of falling prices is followed by a period of reasonably steady growth. But to be really successful, pound/cost averaging does depend on the investor having the wit and timing.

If you are to get out before prices slumps again, the effects of pound/cost averaging will fade because markets are always, historically at least, on a rising trend. Some investors argue that putting a lump sum into a market, even when it appears to be on an overvalued peak, will always provide a better return over the long term than doling out money gradually, as short-term highs are invariably exceeded over the longer term.

Preference shares

In addition to issuing *ordinary shares**, a company can issue preference shares to raise capital. 'Pref shares' are less risky than ordinary shares in a number of ways. First, they are entitled to a *fixed dividend**, whereas the dividends paid on ordinary shares are variable and can be cut or waived in years when profits are low.

Secondly, preference shareholders are entitled to receive their dividend before ordinary shareholders. Thirdly, if the company is wound up, preference shareholders come before ordinary shareholders in the pecking order for repayment. However, in both respects, preference shareholders rank below *loan stock** and *debenture** holders. And although the preference share dividend is fixed, it can still be waived if the company runs into difficulties.

Preference shares can be bought through a *stockbroker**. There are also *unit trusts** which invest specifically in preference shares, and others that invest in them in combination with other instruments such as *convertibles** or *bonds**. Preference shares and funds that invest in them can be held in personal equity plans (*PEPs**).

Variations on the preference share theme are *zero dividend preference shares**, which receive no dividend but give a predetermined capital gain, and *stepped preference shares**, on which the dividend increases by a fixed amount each year. Both types are found in split *capital investment trusts**.

Another variation on the theme is the convertible preference share, which can be converted into an ordinary share within a certain period or on a certain date.

Price/earnings ratio

The price/earnings ratio (p/e ratio) is an important tool for company analysts and it shows what a company earns relative to its *share** price. The ratio is calculated by dividing the share price by the *earnings per share**. If a company's share price is 600p and its earnings per share in issue are 50p, then the p/e ratio is 12 (600/50 = 12). In other words, the company's share price is 12 times earnings.

As a general rule, the higher the ratio, the faster the rate of growth the stockmarket expects in the future. A high p/e ratio often suggests a growth company whose earnings are small but whose shares are in demand because the company is expected to expand. A low p/e ratio often suggests a company with a more stable outlook, or one in a high-risk area. But a p/e is only a useful tool if taken in context. Firstly, a company's p/e should be considered in the context of those of other companies. And secondly, if a company's p/e seems to be higher or lower than other companies in its sector, then you should find out the reasons why, because it may be an exception to the generalised rules above.

Primary market

Securities are said to be in a primary market when they are sold for the first time, e.g. through a flotation or placing. Dealing in shares after they have been issued is known as the secondary market.

Private bank

In its original sense, a private bank was a privately-owned financial institution often owned by one family. However, as such institutions have died out or been taken over, private banking is used to refer to a bank's premium service aimed at high net worth individuals. As well as the usual money transfer services, private banking can embrace *portfolio management**, tax and estate planning. Customers are usually assigned a personal manager to deal with the day-to-day administration of their account but pay an annual fee for this higher level of service.

Privatisations

The process of turning public utilities and services into private companies, which the Conservatives began in the early 1980s, has brought many people their first taste of *share** ownership.

The first really popular privatisation was that of British Telecom, whose shares were floated on the *Stock Exchange** in 1984. This was followed by British Gas in 1986 and the regional water and electricity companies which became plcs in 1989 and 1990 respectively. The main area of privatisation in the 1990s has been the sell-off of British Rail, leading to the formation of companies such as Railtrack.

Privatisations have given many private investors their first taste of direct equity ownership, and huge TV and press campaigns were used to encourage small investors to apply for shares. Investors were given an extra incentive to subscribe to privatisation shares with the introduction of *PEPs** in 1987, which meant that shares could be held tax-free and didn't need to be declared on a tax return.

The scope for privatisation in the UK is now limited. Consequently, investors are now looking to Europe where, many analysts believe, there will be an accelerated sell-off of state-owned industries and utilities over the coming years.

ProShare

ProShare was launched in 1992 to promote the benefits of *share** ownership, and it has the backing of all major political parties. It is funded by the *Stock Exchange** and British companies, and seeks to represent the views and concerns of private investors, and to increase public understanding and appreciation of stockmarket investment. One important way in which it does this is through publishing booklets on, for example, how to read company reports and accounts, and on the stockmarket. It also runs seminars and conferences for private investors, and provides services for *investment clubs**. ProShare can be contacted on 0171 394 5200.

Prospectus

A document issued to prospective investors in a new share issue, so they can decide whether it is a good investment prospect. Copies are available from *stockbrokers**. If the company is substantial it will also usually publish the prospectus in the press, normally taking up full pages of the *Financial Times*.

The prospectus will detail the new company's activities and its management, its financial history and may give forecast of future earnings. The information in a prospectus is stringently governed and there are weighty fines for giving false information.

Nevertheless, the company will do all it can to place itself in as good a light as possible and investors should get the view of independent analysts to get a truly balanced picture of the venture.

The prospectus will include an application form for purchasing shares, which can be sent off with a cheque for the relevant amount. No stockbroker's commission is payable nor any stamp duty. However, prospective investors won't know until after the initial offer how many shares they are to be allocated. If the offer is oversubscribed, an investor may get many less shares than they requested. See also *New Issues**.

Public Limited Company (plc)

Any company quoted on the UK stockmarket, either the main market or *AIM** will have plc after its name. Public indicates that its shares are available for purchase, and a plc must have share capital of at least £50,000. Limited refers to *limited liability** and shareholders have no responsibility for the company's financial state, beyond the capital they have put up to buy its shares.

Quotation

The representation of a company on a *stock exchange**, allowing its shares to be traded and giving the company the right to use the marketplace to raise further capital.

Quoted company

A company whose shares are traded on a recognised *stock exchange**.

Real time

Used in reference to stockmarket indices and stockmarket information services which are updated rapidly enough to practically reflect changes on the stockmarket as they happen. The *FTSE 100** index of the UK's leading shares is considered a real-time index as it is recalculated every 15 seconds.

Recognised Professional Body (RPB)

An organisation registered to regulate its profession. RPBs include the Chartered Association of Certified Accountants, the Institute of Actuaries, the Institute of Chartered Accountants in England & Wales, the Institute of Chartered Accountants in Ireland, the Institute of Chartered Accountants of Scotland, the Insurance Brokers Registration Council, the Law Society, the Law Society of Northern Ireland and the Law Society of Scotland.

RPBs can regulate investment and financial planning business carried out by, for example, solicitors and accountants, provided it is not their main activity. If such business represents a sizeable proportion of a firm's activites, it must be regulated by the *Financial Services Authority**.

Recovery stocks

There can be many reasons why a company, or its *share** price, performs badly. There can be problems specific to a company, such as cashflow problems, the loss of a major customer, or poor management; or there can be problems in the wider economy which cause sales to fall or the price of raw materials to rise, or the cost of borrowing to increase. Any of these might cause the share price to fall.

If some of these problems disappear, the company's performance and its share price might recover, possibly sharply. Shares in these types of company are known as recovery stocks, and they fall into two main types: those companies with specific problems and those whose problems are more related to the economic cycle.

As well as trying to spot individual recovery stocks, it is possible to invest in *investment funds** that specialise in this area, both in the UK and in overseas stockmarkets. Recovery stocks, and trusts that invest in them, can be volatile in behaviour because some recovery stocks never recover at all, but instead go from bad to worse.

Redemption

The redemption date is the date on which a redeemable *bond** or *preference share** is repaid. In newspapers like the *Financial Times, stocks** are classified according to their redemption date. The redemption value (i.e. the amount that is repaid) is fixed at the time of issue.

The redemption *yield** (also called the total yield at redemption or the projected total yield) of a bond or stock gives an idea of an investor's total returns from that holding. It shows the return based on the current price (not the price at issue) and takes into account the interest payments and any prospective capital gain or capital loss at redemption. Because prices of these stocks can fluctuate, so too can the redemption yield.

The redemption yield is not the same as the income yield. If you pay more for a bond than its redemption value, the redemption yield will be lower than the income yield; if you pay less, the redemption yield will be higher.

Registrar

The organisation or individual which maintains a company's share register. It is the job of the registrar to remove the names of people which have sold their shares, and add new shareholders, detailing the amount of shares they possess. The registrar is also responsible for a lot of the paperwork sent by companies to shareholders, such as dividend payments, tax vouchers and yearly notification of conversion rights to *convertible** stockholders and announcements of scrip issues.

Most banks offer registrar services, acting on behalf of hundreds of different companies. The name and address of the registrar for a company can be found in its *annual report & accounts**.

Small companies may not use an outside firm; instead the share register is maintained by the company secretary.

Registered securities

*Shares** or bonds where ownership is recorded on a central register, as opposed to *bearer securities**.

Regular savings plans

Investing in the stockmarket was once the province of those with a few thousand pounds to spare. Those savers without a lump sum who wanted to put aside money each month were confined to traditional savings institutions such as building societies or friendly societies. But today this is not the case. The investor with as little as £25 a month to invest can gain access to the stockmarket through the regular savings plans operated by *unit trusts** and *investment trusts**.

A large number of fund managers operate regular savings schemes, although their minimum requirement varies. Some managers accept £25 or less a month, while with £50 a month you have a much wider choice. A few have a much higher minimum of £250 or £500 a month, while a few managers do not accept monthly contributions at all.

As well as making equity investment accessible to those of slender means, regular savings schemes have a number of other advantages. The fact that the money is drip-fed gradually into the investment, rather than all in one go, means that you don't need to worry so much about market timing, or the risk of buying shares just at the moment when they are about to plummet in value. In addition, regular savers benefit from an effect called *pound/cost averaging**, which means that, over time, the average amount paid for the shares works out to be less than the share's average price. This effect is most visible in volatile markets.

Regular savings schemes do have drawbacks. It takes time to build up a sizeable investment. Furthermore, you are never going to experience the dramatic returns enjoyed by those who invest a lump sum just before the share price is about to shoot through the roof. But this is a possibility small investors may be willing to forego, for the sake of having a convenient and easily affordable investment.

Regulation

The regulation of investment business has undergone more scrutiny over the last decade or so than any other area of professional life.

Investors are protected by a regulatory framework which polices a firm's conduct with its clients, the training of its personnel and its financial strength. In addition to this there is a strict system by which investors can complain, including a series of ombudsmen, and a compensation scheme if a firm goes out of business.

The cornerstone of the system was laid by the 1986 *Financial Services Act**, which created a system of regulating bodies, headed by the *Securities & Investment Board**.

This system is now being revised by the Labour Government, which argues that having a number of different regulatory bodies confuses consumers, adds to bureaucracy and makes it easier for miscreants in the industry to disappear, only to resurface elsewhere in the City in another guise.

Labour's solution has been to replace the *SIB** with the *Financial Services Authority**, with the intention that the FSA will cover a wider range of financial organisations, including the regulation of banks (previously controlled by the Bank of England). It will also, in time, absorb the assisting self-regulatory organisations, the *PIA**, *IMRO** and *SFA**, having taken on board a widespread view that self-regulation is not the most effective way to police financial companies.

Retained earnings

That part of a company's profits which is not distributed to shareholders as *dividends** but kept back to fund business expansion.

Reverse takeover

The buying of a large company by a smaller company or, more commonly, the purchase of a *listed company** by a private company, thereby allowing it to quoted on the stockmarket. A reverse takeover can provide a relatively cheap way of becoming a *quoted company** as the acquiring company does not have the initial costs of coming to the market. However in the UK, the acquiring company must demonstrate that the purchase of the company is compatible with its own business activities.

Rights issue

If you hold shares in a company, you may be invited to take part in a rights issue. A company will make a rights issue if it needs to raise more capital, but does not want to borrow the money. Instead, it will give shareholders the right to buy new shares in proportion to the number of shares they already own, so a two-for-five issue means that for every five shares the investor owns, he or she can buy another two.

Unlike a *scrip issue**, the shares in a rights issue are not free. However, the investors can buy the new shares without paying *stamp duty** and without going through a *stockbroker**, so the purchase is cheaper. In addition, the company may price the shares at a discount to the market price in order to make sure the rights issue is fully subscribed. The pricing of a rights issue is a complex issue, because the company has to take into account the impact on its *share** price of diluting the value of the shares already in issue. The share price usually falls when a rights issue is announced because of the dilution.

Around the time of a rights issue, the company's shares are described as cum-rights or ex-rights. Cum-rights means that anyone who buys shares in the company will be entitled to subscribe for the new shares; on and after the date of the new issue, shares become ex-rights, and the right to the new shares stays with the seller.

If you do not want to buy the new shares, you can sell the rights through a stockbroker, since these are traded in a similar way to *warrants** and *options**. If you do nothing, the company is likely to sell them for you and send you the proceeds if there is any profit.

RNS

The Regulatory News Service operated by the London Stock Exchange to ensure that price-sensitive information from its quoted companies is collected and broadcast to RNS users at exactly the same time. The RNS covers news of company results, acquisitions, intention to raise capital, change of directors and key personnel and large shareholder movements.

Rolling settlement

After a *share** deal has been made, settlement has to take place. This is the process of paying for the shares if you have bought them or of collecting the money if you have sold them.

After a share deal is made through a *stockbroker** or share dealing service, you receive a *contract note** from the stockbroker, setting out the terms of the deal, the price and so on. The seller sends the share certificate and a signed transfer form to his or her stockbroker; the buyer sends a cheque for the requisite amount, including *stamp duty** and commission. Settlement day is the day on which the money changes hands.

Until July 1994, settlement was a relatively leisurely affair since it was based on the 'account period'. The year was divided up into fixed two-week *stock exchange** account periods, and any transactions that took place within a certain account period had to be settled on the Monday following the end of the account period (i.e. six business days later). This meant that someone who bought shares on the first day of an account period had three weeks to pay for them.

However, mid-1994 saw the introduction of rolling settlement. This meant that, in effect, every day of the working week was a settlement day. From July 1994 until June 1995, there was a system of ten-day rolling settlement, which meant that settlement had to take place ten business days after the deal. In June 1995, this was reduced to a system of five-day settlement, and there is an intention to reduce this at some stage to three days.

The transition to rolling settlement has made share-dealing more demanding on private investors because it gives them less time to respond to the contract note or pay for the shares. There is hardly any margin for error in the turnaround of documents or cheques, and people in out-of-the-way areas where postage can occasionally be slow may find it difficult to meet the deadline even if there are no errors. However, there are a number of solutions available to the private investor.

The first is to use a *nominee account**. You hand over custody of the share to the stockbroker, who may also operate an interest-bearing deposit account for you so that cash is always readily available to pay for share purchases. Before agreeing to a nominee account, check with the broker about their arrangements regarding voting rights, attendance at *annual general meetings**, and the receipt of *annual reports and accounts**, if these matters are important to you. Also, ask about the security of your money and shares in the event of the firm running into financial difficulties.

Alternatively, you can become a *sponsored member** of the electronic share-dealing system *CREST**. Here, the shares are held in electronic, or 'dematerialised', form in the investor's own name and as such are eligible for all the rights of legal 'on register' ownership.

Rule 4.2 companies

Shares in many of the companies listed on the Alternative Investment Market *(AIM)**, were previously dealt under Stock Exchange Rule 4.2.

The original purpose of Rule 4.2 was to permit trading in companies whose shares had been suspended or delisted. It allowed shares to be traded on a 'matched bargain' basis and, since shares were not listed, requirements were light, for example companies did not have to publish a prospectus.

Over the years, Rule 4.2 grew so it almost became an unofficial market in its own right. However, the launch of AIM has now brought the story of Rule 4.2 trading (and of the *Unlisted Securities Market**) to a close, for companies traded under the Rule were told by the *Stock Exchange** that they must join the main market, or AIM, or be traded off-market. Now the market is only for occasional dealings in companies whose shares have been suspended.

Russell 2000

The principal index of smaller companies in the US, provided by the Frank Russell Company, which follows the next 2000 after the 1000 largest-capitalised stocks on the American market. The constituent shares are reviewed once a year in July to see who's in and who's out.

Scrip issues

A scrip issue, also known as a capitalisation or bonus issue, occurs when a company issues new shares to its existing shareholders, which they do not have to pay for. In a two-for-one scrip issue, existing shareholders receive two new shares for each one that they own.

The object of making a scrip issue is not to give free shares to shareholders, but to make the shares more marketable. If a company operates successfully for a number of years, it may have a relatively small *share** capital compared to the size of its profits, with the result that its share price becomes 'heavy', say £10 or more. Companies fear that this makes the shares less liquid and the scrip issue is an accounting exercise that creates a larger number of lower-priced shares.

The shareholder does not actually profit from a scrip issue, because the shares fall proportionately in value after the issue of the new shares. So on the two-for-one issue above, if the original share had been priced at 900p, the shareholder would end up with three shares priced at 300p each. Any scrip issue proposed by a company must be approved by shareholders, and voting may take place at the *annual general meeting**. If the issue is approved, the company sends out allotment letters to the shareholders. The shares are then quoted 'ex-cap', i.e. at the new lower market price. If you buy the share 'cum-cap', it means the scrip has been approved, but the price has not yet been adjusted.

SEAQ

The Stock Exchange Automated Quotation system, or SEAQ, is a computerised information system that means *stockbrokers** all over the UK have equal access to information about the *share** prices being quoted by *market-makers**. In the days when shares were traded on the floor of the *London Stock Exchange**, the availability of the prices at which *jobbers** would buy or sell could be haphazard – stockbrokers did the rounds of jobbers on the floor, and then relayed the information about what they were quoting back to their offices.

Since *Big Bang**, *market-makers** have fed the prices at which they are prepared to deal into SEAQ. Stockbrokers can then call up a particular share on their screen and see the prices at which different market-makers, identified by a four-letter code, are willing to buy or sell. To make life easier for the broker, the screen includes the 'touch' – the current lowest buying and highest selling price on offer from market-makers, highlighted on what's known as the *Yellow Strip**.

An accompanying system, SEAQ International, details prices for non-UK equities.

Secondary market

The market for a stock or *share** once it has been issued. A share or bond is in its primary market when it is first open for subscription. *Stock exchanges** act primarily as secondary markets.

Securities and Futures Authority (SFA)

The self-regulatory body for *stockbrokers** and dealers in securities and *futures** and *options**. The SFA was created in 1991, through a merger between the Securities Association and the Association of Futures Brokers and Dealers.

The SFA, which covers most member firms of the *Stock Exchange**, is responsible for monitoring behaviour and laying down codes of conduct for its members. It is also responsible for investigating complaints against firms from members of the public. The duties of the SFA are to be absorbed by the new 'super-regulator', the *Financial Services Authority**.

Securities & Investment Board

The erstwhile chief regulator for the financial services industry. SIB was replaced by the *Financial Services Authority in 1997, when Labour came to power. While many of its functions and activities are identical to SIB's, the FSA is intended to cover a wider range of financial institutions.**

Securities Institute

The professional body which sets the Registered Representative Examination, the basic qualification that all *stockbrokers** must possess. Most stockbrokers go on to achieve other qualifications. Most highly regarded is the Securities Institute Diploma. This requires brokers to sit three papers in areas such as private client investment management, fund management and bonds markets, and takes 18 months to complete. The broker must also have three years' professional experience. Brokers who have passed the

Diploma and have become members of the Securities Institute will have MSI(Dip) after their name.

Security

A security is a financial asset, such as *shares**, *government stock**, *debentures**, *bonds** and *unit trusts**. It does not include insurance policies. A marketable security is one which can be traded on a *stock exchange**, such as stocks and shares; a non-marketable security is one which cannot be bought and sold on a stockmarket, for example National Savings certificates and bonds. Listed securities simply refers to stocks, shares and bonds which are quoted on a recognised stock exchange.

Securitisation refers to the process of changing a loan, which is not classed as a security, into a security. For example, if an investor lends money to a person or organisation, and receives an IOU in return, the investor can sell that IOU to someone else, who can reclaim the money later, or sell the IOU to a third party. The IOU is a marketable security and the loan has been securitised.

SETS

The Stock Exchange Electronic Trading Service, which made its debut in the market on 20 October 1997. SETS was introduced to transform the *London Stock Exchange** from the quote-driven market created by *Big Bang** to an order-driven market.

In a quote-driven market, *market-makers**, who act as intermediaries quote the prices at which they will buy and sell, and this information is relayed to brokers via *SEAQ** screens.

Under the order-driven SETS system, stockbrokers enter firm prices at which they are willing to buy and sell on the *order* *book**, and orders are matched and executed electronically. It is hoped this will have two advantages. First, by obviating the need for a market-maker, the spread between buying and selling prices, on which these intermediaries relied to make their money, will narrow or even disappear. Before SETS, the average spread on the *Footsie** stock was 6 per cent; this could drop to 1.5 – 2 per cent, if the UK follows other order-driven markets around the world.

Second, because deals are matched blind it is hoped it will achieve better prices for investors than the old system where brokers could be tempted to deal with a market-maker just to maintain a relationship not because he or she was offering the best price for a client.

Initially, only the *FTSE 100** shares are being traded through SETS and the system has to overcome some teething problems, such as wide spreads between buying and selling prices early and late in the trading day. Most brokers offer clients the option to deal via SETS or the traditional way via a market-maker. However, if they opt not to use SETS, they must be able to match or improve its prices.

Self-regulatory organisation (SRO) - see *Regulation**

Settlement

The process, once a deal has been made on a *security**, of transferring ownership from seller to buyer and money from buyer to seller. Under the current system of *rolling settlement**, this process must be completed in five working days.

SFA - see *Securities & Futures Authority**.

Share

For a company, issuing shares is a way of raising capital (other ways include overdrafts, business loans and *loan stock**). For an investor, buying shares is a way of building up capital or of achieving a growing long-term income. In addition, investing in shares has often proved to be a way of achieving capital growth or income growth that outstrips the rate of *inflation**. About 10 million people in the UK own shares.

A *share** is a share in a company, and the owner of a share is a part-owner of that company. There are various types of share, including *ordinary shares**, *preference shares** and *convertible** preference shares, but when people talk about shares, they are often talking about ordinary shares, also known as *equity**. Different types of share confer different rights, for example preference shareholders receive preferential rights to *dividends** and repayment, but they seldom have the right to vote at the *annual general meeting** of the company. Ordinary shareholders have voting rights, but come behind preference shares in the pecking order for income and capital repayment.

After shares are issued by a company, they are traded on the stockmarket. The market value may bear little relation to the original price because it rises and falls according to supply and demand (see *market influences**). But if the company is fundamentally healthy, short-term volatility should be succeeded by a longer-term trend for growth. This is why shares need to be viewed as long-term investments.

Buying individual shares can be expensive and risky for the

investor, and an alternative way of investing in the shares is to buy *investment trusts** and *unit trusts**.

Both ordinary shares and preference shares (as well as unit trusts and investment trusts) can be held in the tax-free shelter of a *personal equity plan (PEP)**, as long as they are quoted on an EU *stock exchange** recognised by the Inland Revenue. *Individual Savings Accounts (ISAs)**, which replace PEPs in April 1999, can also hold shares tax free, although changes to the *tax credit** will mean it will not be so advantageous to holding high-yielding shares in an ISA as it was to hold them in a PEP.

Share exchange

A facility offered by some *investment trust** and *unit trust** managers whereby you can exchange existing *share** holdings for shares or units in the trust. The attraction of doing this is that it allows you to dispose of odd parcels of shares which might otherwise be expensive to sell through a *stockbroker**.

The costs of share exchange schemes vary. There will be a charge for the sale of the existing shares, the initial charges on the purchase of the investment trust or unit trust, and *stamp duty** of 0.5 per cent if you buy an investment trust. A few managers waive dealing commission on the sale of the shares, but most charge £15 or £20 per holding. Managers also differ in what shares they accept in exchange for their unit trust or investment trust. Most restrict the scheme to shares listed on the **London Stock Exchange***, but they may have a narrower limit, accepting only **FTSE 350** (see **Index***) companies. Few accept overseas shares, although it may be worth asking. Occasionally you will come across a manager offering discounted selling charges for a particular category of shares such as *privatisation** issues.

Share exchange schemes are useful, but they should never be the main reason for buying unit trusts or investment trusts. The prospects of that investment (and of those you are selling) are far more important than whether you can save £5 on the sale charges.

Shareholder perks

The main reasons for the private investor to buy shares are the possibility of achieving capital growth through a rise in the share price, and the possibility of receiving a growing income through the *dividends** issued by the company. Another attraction of shares is that some of them carry shareholder perks to act as incentives to private investors. Shareholder perks are usually based on the number of shares owned, with the incentives restricted to those with a minimum holding of shares. In addition, perks are often tiered so that those with more shares get more or better perks.

The range of incentives offered by companies is wide and, not surprisingly, travel and leisure companies and retailers are a good source. For example, British Airways and P&O offer discounted travel, fashion companies like Austin Reed, Burton Group, and Sears offer discounts in their stores, and several hotel, restaurant and brewing groups give money-off vouchers for meals and holidays. A few financial groups discount charges on their products.

The extent of the perks given may vary according to the company's annual results, and they are often announced in the *annual report and accounts**. Because perks may vary, and because the share performance and dividends are likely to be much more financially important than the incentives given, it is not advisable to buy shares purely on the basis of the perks.

Stockbroker* Hargreaves Lansdown publishes a booklet giving details of the shareholder perks available from companies. For details, telephone 0800 850661.

Share shops

To tie in with the spate of *privatisation** issues of the 1980s, the government and the *Stock Exchange** devised share shops – easy-to-use share-dealing services available at high-street banks and building societies aimed at private investors who could walk in off the street, register and deal there and then. Share shops have screens listing the latest prices, and advisers on hand to explain the process to novices, although the share shop service is usually execution-only and advice of what to buy and sell is not generally available.

Share shops concentrate on the most popularly traded shares. AIM* stocks, *new issues** and non-UK shares may not be available. You can identify a share shop by its distinctive black and white bear-and-bull logo.

Short position - see *Long position**

SIB - see *Securities & Investment Board**

Smaller companies

Can refer in the UK to any quoted company outside the *FTSE 100 index** of leading companies, although some *investment funds** which focus on smaller company investment, classify their investment remit as any company within the *Hoare Govett** Smaller Companies or FT SmallCap indices.

Smaller companies are appealing to investors because they are traditionally viewed to have greater potential for expansion than the stockmarket behemoths and can grow their share price more rapidly. However they also come with greater risks – the smaller the company, the more vulnerable it is to a downturn on the economy and rises in interest rates. This is why those without the time or the understanding to invest directly, are often steered towards smaller company *investment trusts** or *unit trusts** which can diversify their risks by investing in a wide range of different smaller companies.

South Sea Bubble

The South Sea Bubble stands as a fine example of herd behaviour when 'sure-fire' investments are offered to an unsuspecting public with inevitably disastrous consequences. This early eighteenth-century scheme to exploit the mineral wealth of South America was given state sanction with the aim of alleviating public indebtedness, and granted Harley, Earl of Oxford, and his company exclusive rights to trade in the South Seas. The company's stock rose meteorically as the public's expectation grew of the mineral resources the company was to extract, and 'me-too' companies soon formed in Change Alley to exploit similarly unproved resources or inventions. These prompted the epigram:

> "The headlong fool that wants to be a swopper
> Of gold and silver coin for English copper,
> May, in Change Alley, prove himself an ass,
> And give rich metal for adulterate brass."

The public eventually discovered, of course, that it was only, at best, 'adulterate brass' to be found in South America and their now less rich metal was soon withdrawn, but not before many, including the directors of the scheme, were bankrupted.

Split capital investment trust

A type of *investment trust** which divides into different classes of *share**, catering for different investment objectives and tax needs. They have their roots in the high tax environment of the late 1960s and 1970s when the desire to find tax-efficient investment vehicles was even greater than it is nowadays.

The first 'splits' had two types of share: income and capital. The first received all the income from the trust's assets during the life of the trust, while the second received no income at all, but at the end of the trust's life they shared the growth achieved by the trust. Investors could choose between the two types of share according to their tax and investment priorities.

Since the 1980s, splits have become complex and have started to offer *preference shares** and highly geared *ordinary shares**. *Zero-dividend preference shares** offer a fixed level of growth which is paid out when the trust is wound up. *Stepped preference shares** pay dividends which rise at a predetermined rate each year, and have a predefined redemption value. Both types are suitable for people who have a fairly low appetite for risk.

Highly geared ordinary shares offer high income and an entitlement to any assets remaining when the trust is wound up.

Of the different classes of share, capital shares are the most risky, since they receive only what is left after the preference and income shares have received their dues. If the trust has performed badly, they will receive very little; on the other hand, as their returns are not fixed, they stand to gain the most if the fund has done well. Highly geared ordinary shares are also high risk.

Splits have a fixed winding-up date, although it is possible to extend the life of the trust beyond that date if the shareholders wish to do so.

Anyone thinking of investing in a split should be careful when choosing which class of share they want, since they are not interchangeable. You also need to look carefully into the trust's performance and prospects, to try to ascertain what its *net asset value** might be when it is wound up. For these reasons, it is important to take professional investment advice when buying splits.

Spread

The *share** prices shown in newspapers are the mid-market price of the shares, but they are not the price at which you would buy and sell them. In addition to the mid-market price, a share will have an *offer price** (the price at which you would buy it), and a *bid** price (the price at which you would sell it to a *market-maker**). The offer price will almost always be higher than the bid price and the difference between them is called the *bid/offer spread**.

This spread is how the market-maker makes a profit on the deal, however since the new *SETS** system of share-dealing is intended to obviate the need for a market-maker, spreads on buying and selling prices are expected to narrow or even disappear in some cases.

Sponsored member

The shorter period for settling share transactions under *rolling settlement** has led to many investors handing their trades through their stockbroker's *nominee account**. However, there is an alternative way of ensuring speedy *share** settlement – by becoming a sponsored member of *CREST**.

Sponsored membership has an advantage over a nominee in that the investor remains the shareholder, so reports & accounts, dividends, notification of *scrip issues** and *AGMs** are sent directly to them, and the investor is the automatic beneficiary of any *shareholder perks**. However, shares are still kept in electronic form rather than certificated form so investors can be sure of meeting settlement deadlines.

To become a sponsored member, you need to deal with a broker which uses the CREST system and offers sponsored membership. The broker must have access to funds for settlement. This can be done, either by notifying your bank to accept instruction from your broker or by lodging sufficient money in the broker's own bank account to meet settlement costs. CREST charges £20 a year per sponsored member and it is up to the broker whether this cost is passed on to you. If you have existing certificated shareholdings, you can ask your broker to dematerialise them so they can be traded under CREST as well.

Stags

Another example of the stockmarket's fascination with using animal imagery, a stag is an investor who makes a quick profit from buying *new issues** and selling them at a premium.

The stag was much in evidence during the government's

*privatisation** drive of the 1980s and early 1990s, since *shares** like British Telecom were priced fairly low and immediately rose in value when dealing opened. The opportunities for stagging meant that many would-be shareholders sent in multiple share applications, using different addresses and applying for shares in the name of the family dog, as well as trying more sophisticated strategies. This is generally a criminal offence.

Stagging can provide a quick profit but short-term investment can be a risky business, since you can never be certain of short-term rises in share prices.

Stamp duty

A tax levied on certain legal transactions which arises when the documentation validating the transaction has been stamped. Stamp duty is charged at 0.5 per cent when you buy (but not when you sell) *stocks** and *shares**, and its extent has diminished during the last decade, falling from a level of 2 per cent pre-1984.

When you buy shares, the tax payable is rounded up to the nearest 50p and collected by the *stockbroker**. Since stockbrokers rarely include it when they describe their dealing charges, you should remember to take it into account. It will be detailed on the *contract note**, sent after a deal has been agreed. On deals over £10,000 there is an additional levy called the PTM Levy, paid to the *London Stock Exchange**, which helps fund the City *Takeover** Panel.

Stamp duty also applies to house purchases at a rate of 1 per cent on house purchases worth over £60,000; 2 per cent on properties of £250,000 or more and 3 per cent on transactions of £500,000 or more.

Standard & Poor's

A US agency which provides credit ratings for *bonds** issued across the world, to indicate how likely the issuer is to repay the bond on redemption. Standard & Poor's is also responsible for compiling the S&P 500, a stockmarket index for the US stockmarket, comprising 425 US industrial shares and 75 stocks in railway and utility companies, and which broadly equates with the UK's *FTSE All-Share Index**.

Stepped preference share

*Preference shares** usually carry a fixed entitlement to a *dividend** from a company's profits. These dividends are paid out before the dividend on *ordinary shares** is determined, so they are a less risky investment vehicle. They also come higher up the pecking order for repayment than *ordinary shares** in the event of a company going into liquidation.

Stepped preference shares are a variation on the same theme, and you are most likely to come across them if you are looking at *split capital investment trusts** since a handful of trusts include them among their share classes. 'Stepped prefs' pay dividends that rise at predetermined rate, and they have a fixed *redemption** value which is paid when the trust is wound up. They still carry some risk, because if the trust performs really badly there will not be enough money to pay the rising dividend or the redemption value, but they carry less risk than ordinary shares.

Stock

One of the confusing things when you first start reading about the stockmarkets is the profusion of terms which seem to be used loosely and interchangeably. So, in an article about the stockmarket, one might come across the terms 'stocks and shares*', 'equities*' and 'securities*', and it is natural to wonder if these are the same or different.

Stock actually has a number of meanings. It can refer to a *fixed interest** security issued by a government, local authority or company (hence terms like British government stock, gilt-edged stock, *local authority stock** and *loan stock**) in fixed units, often of £100. These are traded on *stock exchanges** and prices can fluctuate according to supply and demand.

Just to confuse matters, stock is also the name for an ordinary share, particularly in the US. Thus, a fairly typical US definition of stock runs: "A security representing ownership of a company and entitling its owner to the right to receive dividends". This definition is reflected in terms like *cyclical stocks** and *defensive stocks** which refer to shares rather than to fixed-interest securities.

Basically then, the term is a loose one that can cover either shares or bonds.

Stockbroker

When you buy and sell shares, you are likely to do it through a stockbroker or through the share dealing services increasingly being offered by banks and building societies. Before *Big Bang**, stockbrokers milled around on the floor of the *London Stock Exchange** and bought and sold shares on behalf of clients, through *jobbers**. Nowadays, they deal with *market-makers** using the computer technology installed in their offices. Both jobbers and market-makers are effectively operating as wholesalers, while stockbrokers and share-dealing services operate as retailers (some share dealing services are even known as *'share shops*'*).

There are three types of stockbroking service. The first and the cheapest is *execution-only**, which means that the broker will simply carry out the client's instructions to buy or sell. Next is *advisory dealing**, where the broker advises on share sales and purchases but leaves the final decision to the investor. Last and most comprehensive is the *discretionary dealing** service, where the stockbroker ascertains the client's investment objectives and then makes all dealing decisions on their behalf, notifying the client afterwards or at regular intervals.

What type of dealing service you choose depends on your circumstances. Someone who wants to buy shares and has very little knowledge of the stockmarket or little time to follow it may be better off with a discretionary or advisory manager, but he or she will have to face the fact that these services are likely to cost more than an execution-only service. When choosing a service, it often pays to be cautious about your own share-dealing abilities, and to think hard before eschewing professional advice.

There are also a few other factors to consider when choosing a stockbroker. Does it offer to hold your shares in the form you want (e.g in a *nominee account**, or by becoming a *sponsored member**)? Are their charges competitive with other comparable services? You also need to make sure that the firm is authorised; that you can contact them easily (for example, they have a branch locally, or that you can easily get through when you phone them rather than finding them perpetually engaged); You may also want to enquire whether they offer services like tax advice or other investment management services, such as *PEPs**.

Obviously, if you are choosing an execution-only service, the list of points you need to check is shorter than if you opt for discretionary dealing. If using the latter, you should hesitate before using a stockbroker with whom you find it difficult to communicate, or who does not make a thorough examination of your financial circumstances and aspirations before giving any advice. The cost of a stockbroker's services varies from firm to firm, and even from region to region (regional stockbroking firms are often cheaper than those in London because overheads are lower). Advisory and execution-only brokers usually charge a commission, calculated as a percentage of every share transaction carried out, while discretionary brokers tend to work for an annual percentage based on the size of your portfolio.

The cost of execution-only dealing has dropped in recent years with the introduction, by brokerage houses and some of the high-street banks and building societies, of 'discount dealing' whereby instructions are taken over the phone and effected immediately.

The introduction of *rolling settlement** has altered the way many stockbrokers work. With the advent of five-day settlement, many brokers now require clients to use a nominee account since this accelerates the settlement process.

Stock exchange

A stock exchange is a market for the trading of *securities** such as *stocks** and *shares**. A country may have more than one stock exchange which together constitute its stockmarket.

A stock exchange has two main purposes. It allows companies, governments and local authorities to raise capital by selling securities. The secondary market, which usually accounts for far greater trading volumes, allows investors who have bought these securities to sell them to other investors. The existence of an active market ensures that securities are 'liquid', and it reduces the risk of buying securities because investors know they can sell them again if they want cash.

In the mid-nineteenth century, the UK stockmarket comprised more than a dozen regional stock exchanges, but these closed and amalgamated so that only the *London Stock Exchange** remains. This is now one of the largest (by capitalisation) stockmarkets in the world, beaten only by the US and Japan.

Stop-loss order

An order placed with a *stockbroker** or portfolio manager to sell a *share** (or commodity) if the price falls to a certain level. It is a way of limiting losses in markets that are volatile, and is particularly useful for speculators who may experience difficulty in following the movements of the markets or in contacting their broker.

Stop orders can also take other forms. For example, you can give instructions to the broker to sell a share and take the profits if its price rises to a certain level, or you can give orders to buy a share if its price falls or rises to a certain level.

Strike price

Used in *options** trading – the price at which the buyer of a put option acquires the right to sell the underlying investment to the person who wrote the contract, or, on a call option, the price at which the purchaser of a call option acquires the right the purchase the investment. Also known as the exercise price.

Takeover

The acquisition of a company by another, usually larger, organisation. Many takeovers are friendly, and many smaller companies position themselves to be an attractive target for acquisitive corporations.

A prospective takeover must be put before a company's shareholders. The acquiring company will tempt shareholders to vote for the merger by offering to exchange their existing shares for shares in the acquiring company, or a combination of shares, *convertibles** and cash. If the targeted company is resistant, the predatory company may have to resort to a hostile takeover by purchasing enough stock in it to become a majority shareholder.

However, all bids must comply with rules laid down by the City Takeover Panel. Companies may bid for up to 30 per cent of another company's shares (this is why it is so important to watch out for companies building up substantial shareholdings in other firms; companies often try to take the market unawares by buying shares without warning in a 'dawn raid'). Once its holding reaches 30 per cent, it must make a full offer for all the remaining shares at the highest price paid for shares so far. Once its holding hits 50 per cent, the acquiring company can give remaining shareholders two weeks to make up their minds.

Takeovers are highly regulated. No-one involved in initial takeover discussions is allowed to deal in shares in either company before an offer is publicly made and once an offer is announced, all trades must be reported to the City Takeover Panel. Some takeovers are referred to the Monopolies & Mergers Commission if there is any indication that a company is looking to buy up its rivals to create a monopoly in its market.

Tax

Every individual is subject to three direct forms of taxation: income tax, *Capital Gains Tax** and *Inheritance Tax**. In each case, everyone has a personal allowance, below which no tax will be payable. If you start following the stockmarkets, you will also come across other forms of tax, such as *stamp duty**, *Corporation Tax** and *Advance Corporation Tax**.

The tax most likely to affect the individual is income tax. Everyone, including children, has a basic personal allowance for income tax, and there are additional allowances for married couples, the disabled, widows, and those aged 65 and over. Income tax is levied on your salary (at 20, 23 or 40 per cent depending on earnings), and on investment income such as interest on bank accounts, *share* dividends**, and income from *unit trusts**. Income from investments is usually paid net of 20 per cent tax, and non-taxpayers usually have to reclaim the tax paid (they can register for gross interest on deposit accounts), while 40 per cent taxpayers will have to pay further tax later on, which must be declared on their tax return.

A few investment vehicles, such as *Personal Equity Plans (PEPs)**, *Individual Savings Accounts** (ISA) and TESSAs, are exempt from income tax, while others earn tax relief, which means that the money you contribute is topped up by the government. These include the *Enterprise Investment Scheme (EIS)**, *Venture*

Capital Trusts*, and pensions.

It is also possible to defer paying income tax by keeping your money offshore, for example in an offshore bank account or an offshore fund. Returns are still taxable, but it is possible to defer the tax liability until you are in a lower-rate tax band. Investors can also restrict their income tax liability and make more of their capital gains allowance by investing in *zero dividend preference shares**, whose return is treated as a capital gain rather than income.

The taxation of shares is changing. Along with the phasing out of Advance Corporation Tax, the 20 per cent tax *credit** is being reduced to 10 per cent. After April 1999, the tax credit can no longer be reclaimed by pension funds and non-taxpayers.

Tax credit - see *Dividends**

T+3/T+5/T+10

The period for settling the cost for share transactions on the **London Stock Exchange*** is five working days after the transaction took place. This is referred to as T+5 (i.e. trading plus 5 days). When *rolling settlement** took over from fixed settlement periods, the period was set initially at T+10. It is anticipated that settlement will move to T+3.

Technical analysis

The process of forecasting the prospects for a *share** by looking at movements in its price, trends for earnings and dividends. *Chartists** evaluate shares purely on a technical basis as they believe that stockmarkets move in very precise patterns, but most investors will want to use *fundamental analysis** as well, such as looking at a company's management and products, how the economy is shaping up and who its competitors are.

Tip sheets

If you are an investor trying to get ahead of the herd, it can be very tempting to take out a subscription to an investment newsletter to see which shares are set to rocket in price, giving you the opportunity to make a fast buck. Tipsheets have proliferated in recent years, partly thanks to the easy access offered by the Internet. They can be published monthly or weekly – or even daily on the net.

While tip sheets may promise to let you into the secrets of which shares to buy before anyone else does, remember that you are not the only subscriber and there could be hundreds of other people acting on a newsletter's recommendations, pushing up the share price in the process. Plus, they often get it wrong, although in their advertising they only highlight their winning tips. If they do recommend a dud, you have absolutely no recourse if you lose money.

Of course, newsletters that back up buy and sell recommendations with *fundamental analysis** and serious comment can be worth reading, although this sort of information is widely available in reputable magazines and the City pages of the papers. In any case, canny investors will wait a while before buying on a tip to see how the share price moves. If the company is fundamentally sound, the price will continue to rise after any initial feeding frenzy.

TOPIC

The screen-based service used by the *London Stock Exchange** for providing *stockbrokers** and *market-makers** with the *SEAQ** system of share price quotations.

Traded option

A *derivative** instrument used to hedge bets on the movements in a share or currency. A traded option is a transferable contract written between two parties, which gives the buyer the right, but not the obligation, to buy or sell a particular share, currency or stockmarket index at a particular price at a certain date in the future.

Traded options divide into call options and put options. Call options give the right to buy a share, currency or index while put options confer the right to sell at a certain price. Call options are bought in the expectation that prices are going to rise in order to get the underlying holding at a cheaper price. Put options are bought in anticipation that prices are going to fall in the hope that the 'put' price will be higher than the prevailing price when the time comes to sell.

To buy an option from the party writing it you must put down a margin, usually 10 per cent of the target price. If prices do not go in the direction the holder hoped, the option can lapse unexercised and the maximum the holder will have lost will be the initial margin. Once written, a traded option can be sold on – the price you will get for it depends on the exercise price it is offering, the prevailing price of the share or currency and how long there is left until the strike date. Options are traded on the London International Financial Futures and Options Exchange (*LIFFE**).

For a more detailed explanation, see *Traded Options – A Private Investor's Guide* by Peter Temple (ISBN 07134 8445 4).

Trustees

The legal owner of a trust and endowed with ensuring that all transactions are carried out in the proper way in accordance with the trust deed.

All *unit trusts** must enlist a company, wholly independent from the trust, to act as trustee and its role is administrative as much as anything else. The trustee, usually a well-known bank, must ensure safe custody of the underlying assets in the fund, maintain the register of unit holders and collect and distribute income for the fund, among other things.

Private trusts, such as discretionary trusts set up by parents to protect assets for their children, may appoint an individual rather than a company as a trustee. This might be a solicitor or even the person setting up the trust. However, it cannot be anyone who has any beneficial interest in the trust.

Undated stock

Most *fixed interest** securities come with a fixed redemption date on which the bond issue or par price is returned. But a few have no fixed redemption date but can go on paying income indefinitely. Because of this, the level of income tends to be lower than for dated stock.

Unit trusts

The usual advice for someone buying *shares** is that they should spread their money across at least six to ten shares. Because of dealing costs and commissions, it is not usually practical to invest less than £1,500 to £2,000 in a single share, which means that you need £10,000 at least (and some investment managers would put the figures at £20,000) before you should invest directly in shares. A very useful option for the investor who does not have this amount is the unit trust.

Unit trusts are collective investment schemes that allow investors to pool their money together in a fund. This is managed by professional fund managers, who will buy dozens or hundreds of different holdings. In this way, there should be several benefits for the private investor: professional fund management, cheaper dealing costs, and a more balanced spread of investments.

The fund is unitised, which means units are created every time an investor puts money in the fund and liquidated when he or she withdraws money. If units are worth £1 each and you invest £1,000, you buy 1,000 units, and these will rise or fall in value as the value of the assets held by the fund rise or fall.

There are almost 2,000 unit trusts in the UK, and to make selection easier, they are divided into sectors. These can be geographical (for example unit trusts investing in North America or in Europe) or based on investment objectives (UK equity growth and UK equity income), or the investments themselves (property unit trusts and commodity & energy unit trusts). There are sectors investing in equities, *fixed interest** stocks and cash. Most accept both lump sums and regular monthly savings. Unit trusts are often mentioned alongside *investment trusts**, and indeed, there are similarities between them. Both are collective funds which pool their members' money together, both types of fund can meet different investment objectives such as income or growth, and both can match different risk profiles.

The difference between unit trusts and investment trusts lies in their structure. A unit trust is a fund whose capital is divided into units of equal size, whereas an investment trust is a company whose shares are traded on the *Stock Exchange**. The price of unit trusts is directly linked to the value of the holdings in the trust, while the price of investment trusts is linked indirectly. Unlike investment trusts, unit trusts cannot borrow money.

Unit trusts carry a number of charges. The cost of creating and cancelling units is reflected in the *bid/offer spread**, the difference in the prices at which the manager will sell and buy back units. The spread is usually about 5-6 per cent, which means that an investor who buys £100 worth of units would receive £94 if he were to sell them back immediately, but a few funds have a spread of less than 3 per cent. Unit trusts are also subject to an annual management charge of 1-1.5 per cent.

Deciding which unit trust to invest in can be daunting because of the number available. A common starting point is a UK equity trust or a general international trust. More specialist funds, such as those investing in a single foreign country or one of the more volatile regions of the world like Latin America or the Pacific Basin, are usually better left until a portfolio is large enough to handle the swings in value that these funds can experience.

Your final selection should be determined, of course, by how the fund is expected to perform. One useful guide is past performance, figures for which are given in the *Financial Times* as well as specialist publications like *What Investment,* but you should be aware that past performance does not give any guarantees about future performance. When looking at these figures, you should look for consistent performers – funds which have been in the top quartile of their sector over a number of time periods, rather than one that has been top over one time period, but so-so over the others – as these are the ones most likely to do well in the future.

Unit trusts can be held within a personal equity plan *(PEP)*,* which renders all proceeds free from income tax and *Capital Gains Tax**. However, not all unit trusts qualify for the full annual general PEP allowance of £6,000 (see the entry on PEPs for details). From April 1999, unit trusts can also be held in the PEP's tax-free successor – the *Individual Savings Account**.

Although unit trusts now number in their thousands, many are converting to the more flexible structure offered by an *OEIC**.

Unlisted Securities Market

A 'second-tier' market for those companies which were too small to be listed on the main market. In 1995, many of the USM's functions were taken over by the Alternative Investment Market (AIM)* and the market was closed in 1996.

Unquoted securities

Securities*, such as shares, which are not traded on any stock exchange* are said to be unquoted. Usually this is because the company's market capitalisation is far too small for it to be quoted or because it fails to meet some other requirement.

Two vehicles, the Enterprise Investment Scheme (EIS)* and venture capital trusts*, allow private investors access to unquoted companies in the hope that today's small unquoted company might bloom and grow and provide handsome rewards for its backers . Both VCTs and EIS have extensive tax breaks to encourage investors to back young enterprises. However, because of the nature of the investment, EIS and venture capital trusts can be very volatile and are best treated with caution. You should never be tempted to invest in them purely on the strength of their tax exemptions.

Venture capital trusts

Venture capital trusts (VCTs) were devised in the 1993 Budget as a way for unquoted companies to obtain financial backing, but the rules were not finalised until the November 1994 Budget.

Venture capital trusts are a form of *investment trust**, and their shares are traded on the *Stock Exchange**. They invest in smaller unquoted companies and, possibly, companies quoted on the Alternative Investment Market *(AIM)**, and since these are high-risk, venture capital trusts offer considerable tax incentives.

First, investors who buy ordinary *shares** in a VCT receive income tax relief of 20 per cent upfront, so that in effect a £1,000 investment would cost £800. Second, investors are exempt from all income tax on *dividends** received from the trust, and from all *Capital Gains Tax** on the disposal of shares in the trust (in these respects, VCTs are similar to *Personal Equity Plans (PEPs*)*. Third, they allow investors to defer CGT on assets they already own. If you have made a gain that would attract CGT, but reinvest that gain in shares in a venture capital trust, no tax is payable. So a 40 per cent taxpayer with a taxable gain of £10,000 would be able to invest the full amount in a VCT and escape paying £4,000 in CGT. However, the CGT does become payable when you dispose of the VCT shares.

To qualify for income tax relief, the shares in the trust have to be held for at least five years. There is a maximum investment limit of £100,000 a tax year. There is no minimum, but in practice most trusts are likely to require at least £5,000.

In order that VCTs fulfil their primary function of investing in new companies, the rules concerning what they invest in are strict.

Seventy per cent of the trust's capital must be invested in unquoted trading companies which, once the VCT investment has been made, must have a capital value of no more than £11 million. No holding in a single company, apart from another VCT, can represent more than 15 per cent by value of the trust's portfolio, and at least 30 per cent of its investments must be in *ordinary shares**.

Venture capital investment is a highly-specialised area, and if you are considering venture trusts, you need to find a manager with a long and successful history of financing unquoted companies.

Volatility

Investors must be mindful to tailor their investments to an acceptable level of risk. An important aspect is therefore the level of volatility they can expect to experience.

Volatility expresses how deeply the value of an investment fluctuates in value. Young, emerging stockmarkets experience a high level of volatility, partly because their economic outlook is unpredictable but also because they have a low level of liquidity, with relatively few shares available for sale and purchase. Consequently, small trades can have a large impact on the market's movements. More mature markets such as the UK and US are less volatile. Although the market moves up and down on a daily basis – the swings tend to be more shallow. However, there have been periods when, for example, the UK market has swung aggressively. One period of notably strong volatility on the London stockmarket was in 1992, when the City became extremely nervous about the UK's membership of the European exchange rate mechanism which led to *Black Wednesday**.

Individual shares also experience different levels of volatility. The least volatile tend to be the *blue chips** such as the mammoth UK-listed companies which make up the *FTSE 100 index**. These companies are so minutely analysed that it is very rare for any news to take the market by surprise. Instead, they tend to climb in value in reasonably steady fashion, unless there is some shock news such as a sudden board resignation or the stockmarket as a whole is going through a period of trauma. Conversely, smaller company shares can fluctuate wildly, partly because they are less liquid but also because their shares may be priced lower; consequently a fall or rise of just a few pence in their price can mean a much greater fluctuation in percentage terms.

Investors can reduce volatility within individual stocks by holding a basket of different companies' shares. The easiest way to do this is through a collective investment fund such as a unit trust, which provides a ready-made portfolio of different stocks. Investment trusts can also serve this function but as they are listed companies themselves, they tend to be more volatile than unit trusts. Further some investment trusts are highly *geared** which can cause their price to fluctuate strongly.

Fund managers often provide volatility ratings for their funds. A commonly-used measure is *Standard & Poor's** Micropal volatility rating. This shows the percentage by which the monthly unit or share price of a fund has deviated from its average over the past three years; the higher the figure, the sharper the changes in price month on month. Of course, it is unwise to use the volatility rating alone to assess an investment's level of risk. A fund whose share price steadily falls in value month on month would have a very low level of volatility, although the risk of losing money is very high.

The best way to combat volatility is to invest for the long term. Provided your chosen investment is fundamentally sound, short-term fluctuations in price will be superseded by the long-term trend for share price growth.

Volume

In market-speak, this refers to the number of securities being traded on a stockmarket on any given day. The value of a day's trading is called the turnover. Volumes on mature markets such as the London and New York *stock exchanges** run into millions every day. However, there are times when volume is low and trading is said to be 'thin', typically in the summer months and immediately after Christmas. Volume on the commodity markets refers to the number of lots taken.

Voting shares

A company is answerable to its shareholders, but only those with the power to vote at *annual general meetings**. *Ordinary shares**, or *equities**, carry voting rights. However, there is a type of ordinary share, called A shares or non-voting shares which are identical to ordinary shares in all respects except they carry no voting rights and are therefore cheaper.

A company will state in its articles of association which shares carry voting rights.

Wall Street

The popular name for New York's business district on Manhattan, although the famous facade of the New York Stock Exchange is actually situated at right angles to Wall Street, on Broad Street.

Wall Street came to prominence in the 1700s, when cargo ships coming from around the country and overseas docked on the East River and the goods they unloaded were traded there. The first Exchange to set up was ran like an auction house, with shares sold in lots to the highest bidder. But by the end of the 19th century, a system of *market-makers** had taken hold. This system is still in place today.

When an investor gives an order to buy or sell, he does so through a brokerage firm. The brokerage firm transmits the instruction to the exchange floor where it is picked by a 'floor broker'. He then takes it to the trading post where the share in question is traded (there are 22 trading posts on the New York Stock Exchange) and executes the order via the floor specialist he finds there. Confirmation of the deal is transmitted electronically to the brokerage firm which in turn sends a written conformation to the investor.

As well as the New York Stock Exchange, lower Manhattan is also home to *NASDAQ**, a massive computerised trading market for *over-the counter** stocks. Although it is headquartered in New York, NASDAQ terminals are made available to brokers across America and overseas.

Warrants

Like an *option**, a warrant gives you the right, but not the obligation, to buy a *share** at a certain price (the exercise price) by a certain date in the future. The difference between an option and a warrant is that the latter has a much longer time scale, often running for years rather than months. Also, the shares purchased using the warrants will be issued by the company rather than bought from another investor.

Warrants often accompany a share issue, and they can be traded on the stockmarket in their own right. How much a warrant is traded for will depend largely on its exercise price relative to the share's actual price and how near it is to the expiry date. If it seems unlikely that the share price will rise above the exercise price, then there will be little demand for that warrant. Note that the value of warrants is likely to be more volatile than the underlying shares, and this can be a high-risk area of investment.

Xd

Shorthand used in newspaper share listings for *ex-dividend**.

Yearling bond

A type of *local authority stock** redeemable 12 months after issue.

Yellow Book

Colloquial name for the *London Stock Exchange** 'bible', Admission of Securities to Listing', which sets out the requirements a company needs to meet before it can acquire a *listing** on the main market, and its continuing obligations once on the market.

Yellow Strip

The band on a broker's *SEAQ** screen which highlights which *market-makers** are offering the best price in a particular stock at a given moment in time, known as the touch price.

Yield

The yield of an investment is the return you receive on it relative to the price paid for it. It is expressed as a percentage. The yield on a building society account will be the annual rate of interest you receive on it, while the yield of a *stock** or *share** shows the interest or *dividend** as a percentage of the price paid for it. If you buy shares at 50p each and receive an annual dividend of 5p, the yield is 10 per cent.

The concept of the yield is simple, but it is complicated by the fact that there are different types of yield. It is important to differentiate between them, particularly when buying *bonds**. The nominal yield describes the annual interest payment relative to the par value (the issue price and also repayment value of the bond at *redemption**) and will normally be expressed as part of the name of the bond, for example Exchequer 15% 1999 pays 15 per cent. But because bonds are traded in the stockmarket, at a price which can be above or below the par value, you must also look at the 'interest yield' or 'running yield', which shows the interest rate relative to the price paid. Exchequer 9% 2002 has a par value of £100, but was trading at £113 5/16 on 28 April 1998 so the nominal yield was 9 per cent but the running yield 8.11 per cent.

The redemption yield of a bond or stock gives an idea of an investor's total returns. It shows the return based on the current price (not the price at issue) and takes into account the interest payments and any prospective capital gain or capital loss at redemption. So on 28 April 1998, the redemption yield on Exchequer 9% 2002 was 6.2 per cent (source: *Financial Times*).

Yields are normally expressed gross, that is before tax is deducted from the interest payment or dividend.

Zero coupon bond

Unlike most *bonds**, a zero coupon bond does not pay out interest; instead it offers investors a capital gain (in this respect, it is similar to a *zero dividend preference share**). For example, instead of issuing a bond at £100 and paying 11 per cent interest, a company or local authority might issue a bond at £30 to be redeemed at £100 at maturity. So, in effect, the interest is paid at maturity rather than during the bond's lifetime. For most taxpayers, making a capital gain in this way rather than receiving income may be more tax-efficient.

A 'strip' can work in a similar way to a zero coupon bond. Strips are the *securities** that result if you break up a bond into its different components such as the interest payments and the repayment value. If you stripped a 10-year bond, you might be left with 20 coupon strips (i.e. the rights to the half-yearly interest payments) and one principal strip that would receive the redemption value at maturity. This would be sold at a large discount because of the loss of the interest payments.

Zero dividend preference share

Zeros, or zero dividend preference shares to give them their full title, are a variation on the theme of the *preference share**. Whereas standard preference shares pay a fixed *dividend** out of the company's profits, a zero does not pay any dividend (as the name suggests). Instead, they offer a fixed capital return, because they carry a fixed redemption value. The capital gain may be less than the gains possible on ordinary shares, but there is much less risk attached.

Zeros are suitable for investors who need a fixed capital sum at a specific time in the future, and are often used in school fees planning. They are also tax-efficient for investors who are taxpayers – since they pay no income, there is no liability for income tax. Any capital gain at redemption will only be liable to tax if you have exceeded your annual *Capital Gains Tax** allowance.

They are issued by *split capital investment trusts** and there is a choice of 37 on the market. They can be bought through *stockbrokers** or direct from investment trust managers.

INDEX